Good Schools
The Policy Environment Perspective

UNDERSTANDING EDUCATION AND POLICY

William T. Pink and George W. Noblit, *series editors*

Good Schools
The Policy Environment Perspective

Charles A. Tesconi
The American University

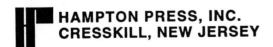

HAMPTON PRESS, INC.
CRESSKILL, NEW JERSEY

Printed in the United States of America

Library of Congress Cataloging-in-Publication Data

Tesconi, Charles A.
  Good schools : the policy environment perspective / Charles A. Tesconi.
      p.   cm. -- (Understanding education and policy)
  Includes bibliographical references and indexes.
  ISBN1-57273-024-2(cloth) --ISBN1-57273-025-0 (paper)
    1. School management and organization--United States.
  2. Education and state--United States. 3. High schools--United States. I. Title. II/. Series.
  LB2805.T44   1995
  371.2'00973--dc20   95-10003
                                                            CIP

Hampton Press, Inc.
23 Broadway
Cresskill, NJ 07626

To Janice
who puts it all in perspective

Contents

PART II: THE SCHOOLS AND A POSTSCRIPT

PART III: THE POLICY ENVIRONMENT PERSPECTIVE

Acknowledgements

This book was several years in the making. George W. Noblit of the University of North Carolina, Chapel Hill, and Professor William T. Pink of National Louis University, editors of the Understanding Education and Policy series, encouraged me to see it through and stayed with me. I thank them for their support and commitment.

I also thank the Graduate Faculty of The University of Vermont. Their approval of a grant proposal allowed me to fulfill the research ambitions I brought to this project. I appreciate, too, the help of University of Vermont graduate students: John Gallagher, Larry Hills, Constance Norris, Maria Sciancalepore, and John Swanson read drafts of parts of the manuscript and helped me to think though some ideas. Thanks also to all those students who listened patiently as I talked about this project. They helped me to sharpen my thinking.

Sharon Briggs, a Ph.D. candidate at The American University, helped me to bring order to PART I, and I thank her for that.

As always, I owe my good friend Donald Warren, Professor and University Dean of Education at Indiana University, an enormous debt of gratitude for his contribution to this book and much more. Don used "policy environment" in referring to an aspect of education policy when he, Professor Mary Anne Raywid of Hofstra University, and I were writing *Pride and Promise* (1985). His idea stayed with me and came to mind during this project. It became more than a label for policy features of the schools; it turned out to be the organizing principle for my study. Don may not agree with the way I have used the term, but I thank him for giving it to me.

I express deep gratitude to my wife Janice to whom this book is dedicated. She endured my tribulations with this project and edited several iterations of the manuscript. Those of you familiar with my writing will note a marked improvement. That is Janice's doing. This book is better for her involvement with it.

I thank Bruce Haslam who was kind enough to get me involved in the Secondary School Recognition Program of the United States Department of Education. That involvement started all this.

I wish also to note the obvious: This book could not have been done without the cooperation of the school professionals, students, parents, and citizens portrayed in this book. They and their schools are designated by pseudonyms in this book, but I wish them to know that their hard work for and their commitment to their schools is a continuing source of inspiration for me.

Though I wish I could claim otherwise, the faults of this book are mine.

Preface

I became involved with the schools depicted in this book through the Secondary School Recognition Program of the United States Department of Education. The program was established to celebrate schools that were unusually successful and those making significant progress in the face of major obstacles. As a site visitor, my task was to substantiate claims about some of these schools. I interviewed students, school professionals, school board members, local government officials, parents, and citizens of the schools' communities. I analyzed documents related to the nature and operations of the schools, examined standardized testing and other student performance data, and I observed various activities in the schools.

The assignment was a welcome break from my administrative duties. As a Dean of a College of Education and Social Services and as a Professor of Education, I dealt with issues concerning schools, but it had been years since I had spent any significant amount of time in them. The assignment offered me contact. I expected simply a change in routine and a chance to see what good schools might be like.

I became captivated. I was inspired by school professionals who gave of themselves beyond dutifulness to work for the success of their students. I marveled at how students, parents and others of the communities served by the schools were extraordinarily complimentary about them. I was intrigued with the relatively high academic performance and college-bound rates of economically poor youth from some of these schools. I became convinced that some of the schools were truly exceptional and worth a long look. Understanding them became compelling.

Thus it was that I began an involvement with some special schools that was to last, on and off, for several years. Some of that involvement had to be direct: To understand the schools I would have to spend some time in them. So, I quit "deaning," went on sabbatical, and set out to study the schools from the inside.

Although I found the schools depicted herein to be exceptional, I make no claim to extraordinary findings. Nor do I possess all the evidence that may be suggested by my speculations about these schools. What you will read here is a compilation of my observations, and some conclusions I have drawn from them.

I do insist that the policy environment perspective grounded in this study and advanced in this book offers a unique, testable, and fruitful way to distinguish among qualitatively different schools. I think, too, that the policy environment perspective illuminates conditions necessary to effect school change and improvement.

I hope I convey also the immense esteem in which I hold those schools professionals who opened their work to me.

Charles A. Tesconi
Washington, D.C.
January, 1994

Series Preface

Books in this series, *Understanding Education and Policy*, will present a variety of perspectives to better understand the aims, practices, content and contexts of schooling, and the meaning of these analyses for educational policy. Our primary intent is to redirect the language used, the voices included in the conversation, and the range of issues addressed in the current debate concerning schools and policy. In doing this, books in the series will explore the differential conceptions and experiences that surface when analysis includes racial, class, gender, ethnic and other key differences. Such a perspective will span the social sciences (anthropology, history, philosophy, psychology, sociology etc.), and research paradigms.

Books in the series will be grounded in the contextualized lives of the major actors in school (students, teachers, administrators, parents, policy makers etc.) and address major theoretical issues. The challenge to authors is to fully explore life-in-schools, through the multiple lenses of various actors and within the anticipated that such a range of empirically sound and theoretically challenging work will contribute to a fundamental and needed rethinking of the content, process and context for school reform.

The book by Tesconi, *Good Schools: The Policy Environment Perspective*, sets out to interrogate ideas generated within the effective schools movement by looking at schools from the inside. By generating case studies of three geographically different schools, each recognized as "good schools" through the President's Recognition Program, Tesconi uncovers both similarities and differences that reveal the problematics of generating uniform policies for schools. We are happy to present this book as the first in the series *Understanding Education and Policy*.

Part I

Context
Approach
Focus

Chapter 1

The Effective Schools Context

Until the mid 1960s few Americans questioned the capacity of public education to deliver on its promises. The 19th century surmise that public schooling was necessary to our way of life, that it ensured access to opportunity, knowledge, broadened vision, and respectability was accepted. If the public school was faulty in favoring whites, in not teaching the basics well, or somehow not functioning well, the public believed it was a mere deficiency readily rectified by an infusion of financial resources, a transfer of teachers and students, or an introduction of innovative methods. Problems were solvable shortcomings, not irreparable crises; the fundamental value and promise of public education was inviolate.

Developments in the 1960s changed that attitude, as they changed so many things. In this case, the occasion was the publication of one of the most important and controversial educational policy studies ever conducted. The study was mandated by the Civil Rights Act of 1964. Section 402 of the act stipulated:

3

> The Commissioner [of Education] shall conduct a survey and make a report to the President and the Congress, within two years of the enactment of this title, concerning the lack of availability of equal educational opportunities for individuals by reason of race, color, religion, or national origin in public educational institutions at all levels in the United States, its territories and possessions, and the District of Columbia.

Directed by sociologist James Coleman et al., this study, entitled, *Equality of Educational Opportunity* (1966), addressed comparability among public schools in the presence and quality of such characteristics as laboratories, textbooks, libraries, teacher experience and salaries, and range of curricular offerings. The study examined the relationship among these "input" characteristics, students' family background, and students' performance on standardized tests of academic achievement.

Coleman and his colleagues found that student family background accounted for more of the difference in students' academic performance than did school characteristics, and that the strong relationship between family background and student achievement endured throughout the schooling years. These and related findings led Coleman to the disconcerting conclusion that schools bring little to bear on academic achievement that is independent of student and parent social and economic background. Coleman did not claim that schools did not make a difference, as some subsequently asserted, but his findings did point to a fundamental problem, presumably in the public school system, and they served to rattle America's faith in public education.

Weaknesses in the Coleman study (see, e.g., Holmes, 1989) may have given initial comfort to those who would indict his findings, but not for long. Among the limitations were overuse of aggregated data and an exclusive focus on school "input" characteristics that were measurable (Holmes, 1989). The aggregated data slighted achievements of individual schools; the focus on measurable characteristics ignored intangible and difficult-to-measure factors such as classroom "climate" for learning or teacher expectations, and these may have affected student performance.

The overall conclusions of what came to be called the "Coleman Report" were soon reinforced, however, by subsequent studies, including an early evaluation of the Elementary and Secondary Education Act (TEMPO, 1968), and by other studies (Ginsberg, 1970; Hanushek, 1972) of schools' effects. Christopher Jencks's *Inequality: A Reassessment of the Effects of Family and Schooling in America* (Jencks et al.,1972) was a powerful affirmation of Coleman's major findings and his general conclusions. *Inequality* was controversial, given Jencks's expressed social philosophy, but it corrected some of the methodological problems of the Coleman study and thus avoided some of its faults.

A Rand-supported study (Averch et al., 1972) summarized for the President's Commission on School Finance the negative implications of all these findings:

> Research has not identified a variant of the existing system that is consistently related to students' educational outcomes. . . . We . . . are not suggesting that nothing makes a difference, or that nothing "works". Rather we are saying that research has found nothing [in terms of schooling] that consistently and unambiguously makes a difference in students' outcomes. (p. 120)

The Coleman study helped to change the way we regarded the concept and practice of equality of educational opportunity. The historic and dominant concern with the place of school "input" characteristics (evoking the argument for equality of conditions) in providing equality of educational opportunity was joined, sometimes displaced, by a concern with the relation between student socioeconomic status and outcome measures (evoking the argument for equality of results vis-a-vis socioeconomic status). This shift gave rise to new debates over resource allocation. Should equality of educational opportunity continue to mean pursuit of the equalization of inputs and, thus, of financing? Or, should it mean an unequal distribution of resources in efforts to make schools serving large percentages of poor children and youth powerful enough to break the connection between students' socioeconomic status and academic achievement?

Above all else, the Coleman study was a major force in challenging convictions about the capacity of the public school to improve the life chances of all children and youth. The American faith in public schooling so deeply embedded in the American ethos was uprooted, never to be the same. This result of the Coleman study was disheartening, and yet it was also the occasion for the emergence of the effective schools movement.

Klitgaard and Hall (1973) mused:

> Perhaps educational researchers had looked in the wrong places for evidence of effectiveness. Previous studies . . .

indicated that, on average, school policies do not greatly affect measurable student scholastic and occupational performance. Suppose this is true. Might there remain, nevertheless, a group of schools that are different? Are there any exceptions to small average tendencies and insignificant regression coefficients? (p. 3)

Klitgaard and Hall (1973) followed their speculations with an examination of outcome data on schools in Michigan, New York City and New York State, and on some special project schools. In the process they found some schools and school districts to be "statistically unusual" ones that appeared to perform better than similar schools and districts.

An early effective school researcher and a popularizer of school improvement through the findings and conclusions of this line of inquiry told a similar story:

My colleagues and I at Harvard University began in 1973 a national research project that very laboriously collected individualized income, social class and family background data on all children in grades 3 through 7 in a large number of schools and school systems in various places throughout the United States. We followed our collection of income and social class data by collecting the achievement data on the same children for all the years . . . they ha[d] been in school. We than analyzed the interaction between those data . . . we wanted to find schools that had . . . abolish[ed] the . . . link between pupil performance and family background. . . . We would nominate a school as . . . effective if . . . it could demonstrate for at least three years before we arrived on the scene its ability to deliver basic skills to the full range of its pupil population. (Edmonds, 1980, pp. 1-2)

Edmonds (1980) reported from his closer look at schools:

We did succeed in finding numbers of elementary and intermediate schools that were consistently effective in their abilities to deliver basic school skills, which we can now call minimum competencies, to the full range of the . . . population that they serve[d]. That was the identification part of the work. (p. 2)

To the question, "Are there schools that shape academic achievement independent of students' socioeconomic background?" (which resulted from findings of Coleman, Jencks et al., and others), Edmonds (1979) and others, (e.g., Brookover, Beady, Flood, Schweitzer, & Wisenbaker, 1979; Brookover & Lezotte, 1977; Klitgaard & Hall 1973; Rutter, Maugham, Montimore, Ousten, & Smith, 1979; Weber, 1971) answered "yes." There were schools sufficiently powerful to overcome students' out-of-school experiences and to make a difference in their performance.

Having located such schools, researchers set out to find out what they were like. They wanted to know if there was something distinguishable about these "effective" schools that might account for their unusual performance. Edmonds (1980) put it this way:

> We did sufficient controls to be certain that . . . [t]here was insufficient variation in the . . . pupil population, the neighborhood or the characteristics under which the school functioned to explain away the dramatic achievement differences that we could consistently find across the city schools that we were studying. (p.3)

Edmonds was to conclude (1979,1980,1982) that the effective schools of his studies were distinguished by:

- a pervasive and broadly understood academic focus or school mission
- frequent assessment of student progress as bases for student and for program evaluation
- teachers with the strong belief that all students could master the curriculum
- a safe and orderly school climate conducive to learning
- a principal with instructional as well as administrative leadership.

"Schools that have these characteristics all together and all at once," he claimed (1980, p. 3), "consistently represent the population of effective schools as contrasted with the population of ineffective schools."

What began as a modest but complicated initiative to locate a few effective schools and their distinctive features became a national treasure hunt. As the effective schools literature grew, so did the traits attributed to effective schools. The Secondary School Recognition Program (SSRP) (see Chapter 3) screened for 14 traits. Brookover, Beamer, Efthim, Hathaway, Lezotte, Miller, Passalacqua, and Tornatzky (1982) created a profile of the effective school that listed as many as 37 or more traits, depending on how one counts. In any case, research generated by the interest in effective schools became mountainous, and it occasioned another nationwide trend. A school improvement movement, undertaken through analysis and emulation of effective schools, was upon us.

By the early 1980s, the claims of the effective schools research were seen as the means to improve schools and to put the bleak forecasts of Coleman and Jencks to rest. The United States Department of Education was sufficiently taken with effective schools research to establish the Secondary School Recognition Program. Educational leaders and public policy makers looked to effective schools research to help all schools meet expectations associated with the school reform movement of the 1980s. Effective schools research and school reform continues today to be uttered in the same breath.

The appeal of the effective schools movement is not surprising. It rests on a compelling idea: School traits said to promote achievement among all children, most dramatically among poor children, can be appropriated by mediocre and bad schools to make them better. What policy maker would not be taken with such a straightforward solution?

Unfortunately, effective schools research and the school improvement movement associated with it suffer from several limitations. Among the major problems is the meaning of "effective" and how to measure it. Pink (1987) cited this as a major flaw. "The most serious limitation of the effective schools research literature is the lack of a single definition of an effective school and standardized instrumentation for measuring the components identified as important" (p. 221). Bossert (1988) agreed. He observed that inconsistent and ambiguous definitions have allowed just about anything to be counted as an indicator of effectiveness, following particular notions of schools as organizations.

These and other problems derived, in part, from the fact that most effective schools research, especially in its early years, was conducted by researchers going into schools and then reporting their observations in the literature. Findings with this descriptive approach are severely constrained by place and circumstance, observer bias, and lack of control variables. The findings were correlational at best and should not be mistaken, as effective schools research and its finding sometimes were in their early years, for model scientific findings or scientific studies and guides for widespread reform. Moreover, much of the effective schools research was undertaken without a well articulated theoretical orientation (Pink, 1987). Research outcomes tended to consist of lists of traits, said to distinguish effective schools from all others, often accompanied by prescriptive rhetoric for attaining effectiveness that lacked theoretical moorings. Grounding in theory is helpful in testing knowledge claims, in building a body of knowledge for follow-up research, and for using research to make recommendations for school improvement.

There were other problems with the effective schools research literature (Purkey & Smith, 1983). Studies and reports of schools already deemed effective tended to slight developments and processes that led up to "effectiveness." Such studies were snapshot-like, taken at a particular time. Working to take on traits attributed to effective schools without understanding how those traits came about could be an exercise in futility. Studying different schools over long periods of time, manipulating and controlling for a variety of variables, and examining differences, similarities, and changes would provide a much better understanding of "effectiveness" and a more credible basis for school improvement (Hallinger & Murphy, 1987).

ON THE OTHER HAND

Limitations aside, effective schools research has taught us a great deal. We have learned that there are disparities in the amount of learning taking place in different schools and in different classrooms in the same school, even after taking into account the skills and backgrounds that children bring to school (Murnane, 1980). Holmes (1989) put it this way:

> There is convincing evidence that there are considerable differences in schools' effectiveness in helping young people achieve specific goals in the basic skills and success in academic examinations. . . . [Further] the evidence is overwhelming that the degree to which the school aggressively works toward academic goals is related to success in achieving those goals. (p. 9)

Holmes also reminded us (1989) that effective schools studies have demonstrated that the following traits do indeed relate to school effectiveness:

- an academic climate of high expectations
- discipline applied universally and fairly
- an orderly and safe atmosphere
- regular monitoring of achievement
- frequent and immediate rewards for good performance
- strong community support
- strong leadership

It must also be acknowledged that effective schools research was an imaginative response to the disconcerting findings and implications of the Coleman and the Jencks studies. Also, it served to remind us about some important social ideals associated with the public school. If fair opportunity is necessary to our way of life, and if public education is a necessary means to that opportunity, then the effective schools research is important simply on its face. Ralph and Fennessey (1983) put it this way:

> The significance of the effective schools research . . . [may lie] more in the ideology underlying it than in the validity of the empirical support for the idea that schools can lessen the effects of race and social class on academic achievement. This idea is crucial to our commitment to schooling as an egalitarian force in modern society. (p. 693)

Finally, it should be noted that the effective schools research and movement did not simply fade away. Studies of schools' effects are not unrelated to effective schools research and the currently popular and dominating force in school improvement; "restructuring," (Elmore & Associates, 1990), with its emphasis on school-site management and authority, is a direct descendent of the effective schools movement.

The study that is the basis for this book falls within the effective schools genre. It is descriptive. It is motivated by my desire to understand public high schools that are deemed successful by many groups: the professionals in them, local school and governmental officials, clients—students, parents,and communities—as well as by the data analyses and review processes of the Secondary School Recognition Program of the United States Department of Education.

This study suffers from some of the shortcomings of the effective schools research. It certainly is limited by observer bias, absence of control or comparison schools, idiosyncratic definitions, and it is a study bound by time and place. However, claims made relative to specific "traits" that should be emulated by less effective schools are modest.

This study moves beyond (or beneath, or behind) school traits. It focuses on norms and choices that undergird traits, give direction to schools, and govern the behavior of the people in them. The norms and choices are expressed through "policy elements" unique to each school that constitute a special, school-based "policy environment." This policy environment perspective illuminates issues that must be engaged if we are to learn from successful schools and apply what we have learned to others.

The policy dimension of this study argues that it is above all else the beliefs, values, and choices—the educational philosophies—of school professionals at the individual school level that grant meaning and governance to goals, direct the behavior of the people in each school, and determine what kind of school change and reform can be accommodated and, thus, realistically considered.

The findings of this study suggest that the attributes of school success made known by the school effectiveness literature are manifestations of something more fundamental and hitherto ignored or given short shrift. It is the school professionals' beliefs, values, and choices converted into policies that result in the manifestation of those traits.

Chapter 2

A Shaky Start

Around midnight on a moonless September night, I found myself driving on empty county roads in the area of the school I was to visit and study. I was looking for a place to stay in these northernmost reaches of New England.

The only places open were gas stations. They were not the sort we see on today's interstate highways, but 1950s rural vintage types: Concrete pillars supporting an inverted V canopy over pumps once topped by lighted globes, the canopy attached to a squat, truncated A-frame building.

My eyes were bleary and my back ached. Why hadn't I taken the advice of the rental car agent back at the airport, almost three long hours south?

"You should stay here," she had said. "It will be midnight at least by the time you get up near . . . [Ruraldom]. There aren't many motels there. Those there close up early. Stay here and drive up tomorrow."

I should have listened, but I wanted to be at the school to witness the start of a school day. About 1 o'clock in the morning, I finally came upon and pulled into a gas station that was open. I asked the attendant what he could suggest for a place to stay. He confirmed my guess; there was nothing for miles.

"If you find a motel it will probably be locked up tighter than a drum anyway. They don't expect people to be driving around looking for a place up here this time of night. I have a room out back that I rent out to stray truckers sometimes. You can use it, if you want. Only twenty-five dollars. No great shakes, but it beats the car."

I agreed, with thanks.

"Glad to do it. Just park on the side of the building over there and walk around back. When you get squared away, come in the front here and have a soda or coffee, if you like. Got a pot going all the time."

I parked as he directed, walked to the back of the building, and entered the unlocked room. I was not likely to get to sleep for a while, so I went around front for a soda.

Three scruffy-looking characters were in the room with the owner. They were drinking coffee, talking loudly and earnestly, slurring their talk. "They've had a night on the town," I thought to myself. They eyed me and my black pin-striped suit suspiciously.

One of the men leaned over to me, his finger poking into my chest as I was reaching for a diet coke in the cooler. "You've got some nerve coming in here, mister. If I were you, I would get the hell out of here and the area, fast as I could."

"Why?"

"We just got the word today, that's why. Dozens of us let go. You suit types don't give a damn. You just sit in Boston and figure the bottom line. That's all that matters to you. Lay off people to save a few bucks. To hell with us and our families. We won't have money to eat!"

He slammed his balled-up fist on the counter. His friends seemed to be getting frustrated with his talk and were, if possible, more hostile yet.

"The hell with him. I want to punch him," said one of the men as he came toward me, the coffee in his plastic cup splashing onto my suit.

I stepped back quickly. "Look, I don't know what you're talking about. I'm not from Boston. I'm here to do some work at the high school, . . . [Ruraldom Union]. Starting tomorrow." I took off my glasses and put them in my pocket, prepared to make as quick a retreat as I could. I wondered if I could get around them before they could react.

"What kind of work?," growled the one who had spoken first.

"Trying to understand what makes the school tick, why it seems to be so good."

I explained that I was there to begin visiting in and studying Ruraldom Union High School. I talked fast, saying that I had been there as a visitor for a federal program that had brought national attention to the school, that I'd kept in touch with the principal and gotten updates on the school's progress, and that it seemed to me to be a very special place, one that I wanted to know more about.

"What do you mean, visiting in and studying the school?," asked the finger poker.

I explained that I wanted to learn as much about the place as I could and that meant being in the school for a while. "Watching, listening, and talking with the teachers, students and others."

They stared at me for several seconds. A grunt escaped from the one who had poked his finger at me as he spilled some more of his coffee.

"Hell, mister, I'm sorry. We thought you were one of the executives from Boston who've been making the layoffs in the paper mill."

He put down his coffee, turned to me with a slight crooked smile and stuck out a beefy, coffee-wet hand. "I've got two daughters at . . . [Ruraldom], mister. It's a damn good school. I know. I'd have stayed in high school if mine was anything like it. And let me tell you, my girls are loved at that place, and they love it!"

Thus began my extended visit to Ruraldom. The father's words were in my thoughts as I approached Ruraldom Union High School a few hours later.

Chapter 3

Some Background

To convey the reason for and method of my study of Ruraldom Union High School and the other two high schools portrayed here, I need to make clear the process from which my study derives. The Secondary School Recognition Program noted in the preface and Chapter 1 began in 1982 under then United States Secretary of Education Terrance Bell. The purpose of the SSRP (U.S. Department of Education, 1983) was to

> identify and call attention to a national group of schools . . . unusually successful in meeting the the educational needs of all of their students. In seeking successful schools, the program also . . . [sought] schools that . . . overc[a]me obstacles and problems, and . . . continued to concentrate on improvement.

Generally recognized as a political success, the SSRP exists to this day, albeit in a different form. The program has generated goodwill for the schools involved, especially for those selected as "schools of excellence," and has produced a voluminous amount of information on thousands of schools (Wilson & Corcoran, 1988).

The SSRP was in existence only three years at the time the schools I have depicted in this study were identified through it. The process for achieving recognition was complex and arduous, and the criteria on which schools were judged were extensive. I describe the process so readers can appreciate how data and information were generated—and how much there was—prior to my on-site work.[1]

It should be kept in mind that the SSRP was not intended to be nor was it ever claimed to be a substitute for social science studies of schools' effects. The SSRP rightfully relied on such studies and "on a broad set of criteria, drawn in part from the research on effective schools, and on the professional judgments of experienced educators whose views merit[ed] respect" (Wilson & Corcoran, 1988, p. 30).

The schools recognized through the SSRP were not presented as the best secondary schools in the nation. They were schools that had documented good student performance through various output measures, had addressed several additional qualitative and quantitative criteria, and were judged by their students, parents, local school and government officials, state education authorities, and by their own school professionals to be good and successful schools.

---

[1] In the first year of the SSRP, each state was permitted to nominate five schools for each level of secondary schooling: middle, junior, and senior high schools. Forty-four states participated and 496 nominations were submitted. The procedure was modified the following school year. Each state was given a nomination quota that reflected its total population and the number of eligible schools. During 1983-84, 48 states, the District of Columbia, and the Department of Defense Dependent Schools participated, and 555 nominations were received. During 1984-85, states were allowed to nominate as many of their eligible schools as there were representatives and senators representing them in Congress. In that year, 49 states, the District of Columbia, and the Department of Defense Dependent Schools were involved, and 509 nominations were received (see Wilson & Corcoran, 1988, pp. 32-35).

FOUR MAJOR STEPS

Step #1

Schools competing for recognition by the SSRP had to pass through four major steps. The first required that local school officials complete a comprehensive Nomination Form (see Appendix #1). The manner through which nomination forms reached local school district officials or individual schools varied, given different practices among the states during the early years of the SSRP. Some state departments of education identified high schools known to be successful, distributed the nomination forms to the appropriate local education officials, solicited their participation, and selected what they regarded as the best from among those that chose to participate. In other states, state education officials distributed the nomination forms to all local school systems, encouraged widespread participation, and set up processes to evaluate completed nomination forms returned to the state department of education. State departments of education used the completed nomination forms to rate and rank the schools that had completed them, and chief state school officers then nominated schools in their state for candidacy in the SSRP.[2]

The nomination form had four sections. The first section called for demographic data, including the racial and ethnic composition of the student body; social, educational, and economic data regarding students' families; and size of the community or communities served by the school.

In the second section candidates described school policies, programs, and curricula relative to 14 attributes of success. These attributes, derived from the effective schools research, were as follows:

- clear academic goals
- high expectations
- order and discipline
- rewards and incentives for students
- rewards and incentives for teachers

---

[2]USDOE officials expected and encouraged variance among the states in approaches to nominating schools, given diverse state-local school relations. Eventually, USDOE staff worked out a selection process with the states that accommodated the diverse social, political, and economic circumstances through which public schools across this country work.

- frequent monitoring of student progress
- meaningful student responsibilities
- teacher efficacy
- concentration on academic learning time
- positive school climate
- administrative leadership
- well-articulated curriculum
- evaluation for instructional improvement
- community support and involvement

School officials documented their self-descriptions in a narrative to demonstrate how the 14 attributes were satisfied through curricula, programs, policies, and practices. These narratives also allowed school officials to demonstrate their knowledge of research on successful schools. Officials could also discuss the extent to which they employed the findings in their schools.

Everyone associated with the SSRP acknowledged that the skill of the authors of these narratives was important in determining how a school's nomination form fared. U.S. Department of Education officials were sensitive to this aspect of the process and used the site visits discussed below as a minimum screen on this reality.

The third section of the form called for information about recent school changes and improvements. Here local school officials addressed factors contributing to their success and obstacles they overcame in realizing it.

In the fourth section, indicators of success, listed below, were highlighted. Applicants provided statistical data and information about their schools in these areas:

- student performance on standard achievement tests
- student performance on minimum competency tests
- post-secondary, college-bound, and related rates
- post-secondary, vocational, and related training rates
- percentages of students enlisting in the military
- percentages of students finding jobs
- numbers of students receiving scholarships and other awards
- student dropout rates
- daily student and teacher attendance rates
- rates of suspensions and other exclusions
- awards/recognition for outstanding school programs
- awards/recognition for notable student achievements
- student awards in competitions (e.g., science fairs)

These indicators, as with the attributes listed earlier, reflected the influence of the school effectiveness literature on the SSRP. Their presence also reflected efforts of the U.S. Department of Education to obtain as much outcome or performance data as possible.[3]

The output measures evoked by the indicators of success were important in the selection of schools to be recognized by the SSRP, but they were not the sole determinants of success. SSRP staff insisted on multiple qualitative and quantitative criteria in this regard, as reflected in the nomination forms and Site Visit Guide (see Appendix 1 and Appendix 2). It was also the case that U.S. Department of Education officials were "unable to compile outcome data on all curricular areas or to obtain test data deseg-regated by race, gender, or social class; nor were they able to provide data on the performance of similar schools" (Wilson & Corcoran, 1988, p. 30). These limitations necessarily qualified the place of output or performance measures in judging the suc-cess of the schools, while evoking the need for other measures.

Step #2

Step #2 involved a review of the nomination forms of the schools nominated for SSRP candidacy by chief state school officers. The review was conducted by a National Review Panel (NRP) convened by the U.S. Department of Education. The NRP was comprised of about 18 nonfederally employed persons broadly representative of constituent groups in public education and knowledgeable about schools (Wilson & Corcoran, 1988). The panelists were univer-sity faculty, professional and civic association leaders, state department of education officials, school board members, business leaders, teachers. and school administrators.

The NRP was divided into teams, each responsible for assessing nomination forms from a particular region of the coun-try. Each panelist would identify those schools that appeared to present the best case for successful performance. Congruence of descriptions, documentation of claims, and evidence relative to the attributes and indicators of success were important in arriving at such a judgment.

---

[3]The nomination form assumed the existence of and accessibility to various data bases. This is not always valid. Sometimes such data do not exist. If they do, use of them is not universal. Also, accessibility to data however well maintained in central offices is not always open to building-level professionals, including principals.

At a subsequent session in Washington, DC, individual team members presented their choices to their teammates. Teams discussed these presentations, settled on those schools they thought worthy of continuance in the SSRP, and brought their choices before the full NRP. The full NRP, aided by U.S. Department of Education staff and consultants, debated the merits of each case brought to it through the team panels and ultimately recommended a set of schools to receive a site visit. The NRP's choices reduced the candidate pool to about half its original number (Wilson & Corcoran, 1988).

Step #3

Step #3 consisted of a 2-day site visit to schools that remained as candidates in the program. Each visit was conducted by a U.S. Department of Education-selected education professional. The purpose of the site visit was to verify information, data, and claims that were reported in the nomination forms and to collect additional information about the school, including the way it was perceived. The staff of the SSRP insisted that the views of representatives of the community be solicited because they believed that successful schools are responsive to the unique needs of the communities they serve (Wilson & Corcoran, 1988).

Site visits were organized to allow collection of information from each major constituent group involved with the school. Site visitors conducted structured interviews with students, teachers, support staff, building-level and central administrators, community leaders, school board members, and parents. They asked the same questions of each group (see the Site Visitor's Guide, Appendix 2) and organized their reports to give the responses to those questions. Site visitors were also expected to explore chances for further understanding. The aim was to represent what each group thought about the school, including their own place and prospects in it.[4]

The U.S. Department of Education charged site visitors to be recorders and reporters only. They were not to evaluate what they heard and saw, nor to make overall assessments or judgments. They were to capture as best they could the essential views of the school held by those with whom they met. Half their time

---

[4]Many of the representatives of the targeted interview groups wanted their schools to be recognized, and such wishes undoubtedly shaped their testimony. To the extent testimony about schools was prejudiced by hopes, it was a prejudice applicable in most if not all cases.

was spent observing activities within the school, and half was spent in interviews and in other information gathering activities consistent with their assignment. Site visitor reports consisted of narrative summaries of observations and descriptions of each constituent group's views of the school. The site visits were crucial to the success of the program because they represented the SSRP's only direct view of the schools.

Step #4

Step #4 involved the study by the National Review Panel of site visitors' reports. Site visitors joined the NRP teams to share thoughts about the schools during this fourth step. On the basis of this review and sharing of information, each team made recommendations to the full NRP. After discussion and deliberation, the full NRP then recommended schools to be recognized as "schools of excellence." All recommended schools were reviewed by the Office of Civil Rights to ensure they were in full compliance with federal civil rights laws.

A NOTE OF CAUTION

There are diverse opinions concerning criteria for determining school success. The issue is rendered extremely complex by the difficulty—the impossibility in most cases—of establishing cause and effect relationships between school characteristics and the performance of students, confounded by characteristics of the students.

The effective schools research literature, as noted in Chapter 1, was plagued by lack of definition relative to "effectiveness" and its manifestations. Nevertheless, that research focused on elementary schools, and basic skills as measured by standardized tests were generally agreed on as appropriate measures to be considered in assessing elementary school effects. Realizing even this minimum consensus relative to assessing the effectiveness of high schools is difficult, given the complex mission of the public high school. Thus, secondary school authorities have come to accept the need for multiple indicators of quality for secondary schools, as contrasted with elementary schools. They understand that Americans expect public high schools to serve social, personal, and vocational, as well as the academic needs of all its students. As Goodlad has reported (1984), we Americans want it all from our schools.

Wilson and Corcoran (1988) analyzed the different conceptions of secondary school quality measures held by different authorities and educational agencies. Their analysis led them to several general conclusions about criteria for judging the effectiveness of secondary schools. The following were among them:

> Multiple criteria should be used to cover the broad mission of the secondary school and to avoid distortions that are created by reliance on single measures.
>
> The criteria should include both student outcome measures and indicators of school processes, but the latter should be related demonstrably to student outcomes.
>
> Indicators of "civility," pro-social behavior, or the absence of anti-social behavior should be among the criteria used.
>
> Attendance, participation rates, and other measures of commitment to the school should be included.
>
> Measures of the school's internal coordination and the level of staff cooperation should be examined to assess effectiveness in use of resources.
>
> Evidence of efforts to address problems and of the capacity to adopt new programs or develop new approaches should be considered. (pp. 29-30)

The processes of the SSRP and the criteria for recognition as a school of excellence were such as to evoke data and judgments consistent with these and related considerations of effectiveness. Accordingly, it seems fair to conclude, as did Wilson and Corcoran (1988), that schools selected by the SSRP "may have been more representative of high quality public education than schools selected using narrow criterion measures such as performances of students on basic skills tests or Scholastic Aptitude Test (SATs)" (p. 30).

U.S. Department of Education officials will be the first to point out that the SSRP leaves much to be desired in meeting the demands of a social scientific study of good and successful schools. Neither U.S. Department of Education officials, nor site visitors, nor others associated with the SSRP would claim that the schools recognized by the Secretary of Education were necessarily the top public schools in the United States, or always deserving. Schools that had realized only seemingly modest attainments, if in the face of major obstacles, were recognized, whereas schools acknowledged in some quarters as quite successful chose not to participate in the program. Nonetheless, the schools recognized by the SSRP must be regarded as at least a cut above average. The methods for gathering information were complex and comprehensive. Diverse quantitative and qualitative data were collected and considered in judging the schools. Policies determined which data were to be collected and allowed to influence the judgments of site visitors and panelists. The data collected and the criteria employed in gathering and using them in judgments fit findings about success-ful schools. Moreover, schools in the SSRP, especially those ulti-mately recognized, were among schools endorsed by their stu-dents, parents, by members of the communities served, by local school and government officials, and by state government and edu-cation officials.

Chapter 4

A False Aha!

Of the 500 or so schools that were selected for recognition during my years as an SSRP consultant, seven were schools I had visited. Through my role as a site visitor and my subsequent contacts with selected schools from among the seven, I had the opportunity to evaluate some things I knew about the effective schools research literature and to consider them relative to these schools. I began to document features that seemed to distinguish each school. I also began to collect impressions and documentation regarding features that appeared to be common among the schools. It seemed there were dimensions common to some of these schools that were not readily apparent in others. For example, teachers in some of the schools enjoyed decision- and policy-making functions—professional authority, as I saw it—that teachers in others did not. Some of the schools devoted a great deal of time to ensuring that new teachers and veterans alike understood what was expected of them. They considered induction and continuing socialization activities as important to the maintenance of their schools' way of life and success.

After four years of site visiting and consulting for the SSRP, and after follow-up contacts with some of the schools, I considered further study of some of them. I had the beginnings of a rich data source and, thus, an opportunity to learn about what made some good schools function as they did.

TEACHER PROFESSIONAL AUTHORITY

I decided to identify schools that I could feel comfortable describing as "good" schools with high degrees of teacher professional authority (TPA). As noted above, I concluded that in some of the schools, teachers exercised professional authority over a range of matters quite unlike what was typically the case. I wanted to study TPA. My view of it, to which I return later, was that it had not been examined sufficiently in the effective schools literature or anywhere else for that matter. It seemed to me to be a critical element in the schools I had visited. I saw it as the key to opening an analysis of schools that were successful enough by most measures and that were also immensely satisfying places to be for teachers, students, and community members.

I was not seeking to determine "effectiveness," as that term has come to be used, nor was I trying to conduct a "scientific" study of school success or of the traits that might be common to some good schools. I was after something quite modest. I wanted to use qualitative methods—interviewing, observing, examining pertinent documents—to study the place and function of teacher professional authority in schools akin to Lightfoot's (1983) notion of the "good enough school"—schools that had an established record of respectable student performance, schools with professionals and staff personnel who had a shared sense of school-based identity and pride, schools that recognized their limitations and sought to overcome them, and schools that were continually seeking to improve the pursuit of their ideals and goals. I was also looking for schools that were deemed successful by their students, parents, and communities.

Because I was considering schools recognized by the SSRP, I was confident that the pool from which I would select schools for further study satisfied these "good enough" criteria and, thus, I would be safe calling them good, not in the moral or aesthetic senses necessarily, but in terms of overall performance. I was not using nor do I now use "good enough" to suggest acceptance of schools with second class performances. Rather, "good enough" acknowledges the complexities of settling on a definition of "successful" or "effective" for high schools and reflects the notion that success and effectiveness relative to any one school can only be considered in the light of each school's unique history, demographics, and other contextual matters. This term also acknowledges the limits on the attainment of some ideal of the perfect high school.

Instructed by SSRP's data collection forms, interview protocols, and a catalogue of performance data that I had collected through my initial site visits, I was able to examine performance data that included and went beyond the attributes and indicators of success addressed in Chapter 3. I studied student performance on SATs; standardized tests of academic achievement; college bound, job placement, and military enlistment rates; drop-out, absenteeism, and vandalism rates; courses completed and credits earned by students; individual, collective, and institutional honors and awards; and daily attendance, suspension, and tardiness rates. I also analyzed each school's

- educational philosophy statements
- mission and goal statements
- accreditation and other self-studies
- faculty and student handbooks
- school policy manuals
- operations and procedures manuals
- personnel regulations
- minutes of building-level committee meetings.

Further, my initial site visits and subsequent follow-up contacts with some of the schools provided notes based on numerous hours observing and talking with school professionals, staff, students, parents, school board members, and civic leaders as they participated in diverse policy and decision-making arenas.[1]

THREE HIGH SCHOOLS

I eventually settled on three schools. They had been recognized by the SSRP; embodied my Lightfoot-inspired idea of solid, good enough schools; and the teachers in them exercised professional

---

[1] I eventually interviewed, formally and informally, over 360 parents, 250 students, 400 teachers, 18 principals, 30 assistant or vice principals, over 100 department heads, 35 central administration staff, 18 superintendents, 43 associate and assistant superintendents, and 90 school board members. Some of the interviews were group interviews.

authority over a broad range of matters. Importantly, the professionals and support personnel in these schools made clear their willingness to cooperate with me. Also, the schools functioned in different contexts: one was rural in setting, another suburban, and the third urban. Ruraldom, Townston, and Cityville were natural and telling, if not imaginative, pseudonyms.

I prepared for each extended visit by updating data that had been reported in the SSRP forms and verified by me in my site visitor capacity and by reviewing and updating information and data I had collected through contacts with the schools subsequent to my site visits.

- I studied the rules and regulations intended to direct each school's internal organization and the governance of its members.
- I read anew faculty, support personnel, and student's handbooks.
- I studied minutes of faculty meetings and of standing and ad hoc committees.
- I reviewed my observation notes based on watching as significant actors made decisions and formulated policy.
- I assessed congruency between policy and practice over a range of matters, from the place of school professionals in policymaking generally to the specifics of the design and development of curriculum.
- I considered whether and which qualities of the schools were attributable to building-level decisions.

In short, I prepared for each visit by increasing the breadth and depth of the information I had previously collected.

These preparations affirmed my initial impressions regarding teacher authority. Teachers in these schools enjoyed a high degree of professional authority reflected in the range of matters over which they exercised at least some influence. Teachers were:

- influential in shaping educational philosophy and in establishing school-wide content, learning, and curricular goals
- major contributors to various school-wide long-range and strategic planning and development initiatives
- having a voice in the design, development, and evaluation of school-wide curricula

- playing a decisive role in the evaluation and selection of textbooks
- influential in the selection and in the evaluation of peers and support staff
- major designers of their own in-service and professional development activities.

Teachers in these schools, then, manifested a degree of authority that is not generally accorded to secondary school faculties.[2]

As noted, this feature of some schools that I found impressive and atypical I call *teacher professional authority* (TPA). For this study I define it as:

Teachers' capacity to influence or to determine the educational philosophy of their schools, to help derive school-wide learning goals from that philosophy, and to help fashion the overall policy context through which the goals and school mission are to be pursued.

The evidence I had collected about TPA in some of the schools derived from my examination of statements in various school publications, consideration of the membership lists of standing and ad hoc committees, testimony from various groups, and observations of committees at work and the place of teachers' voice on them.

My reasons for focusing on TPA were largely unexamined. I was impressed by public school faculty who played major roles in determining academic policy. Also, I was intrigued by the contrast between what I saw in some of these schools and what I saw

---

[2]Numerous studies and surveys have documented the absence of a teacher voice in policymaking. Among them: NEA (1986, March), Lou Harris Associates (1985), and The Carnegie Foundation For The Advancement of Teaching (1988, September). The 1985 Metropolitan Life Poll of the American Teacher showed that 41% of the teachers polled by Harris wanted out of teaching because they lacked a voice in the shaping of the policy environment within which they had to pursue others' goals (reported in Education Week, September 25, 1985, p. 6.). Another poll of 8,500 elementary school teachers, conducted by *Instructor Magazine* (reported in *Teacher Education Reports*, April 24, 1986) for William Bennett, former United States Secretary of Education, revealed that 80% of those surveyed cited increased teacher involvement in curricular decisions as central to school improvement and teacher satisfaction. Almost 85% cited increased teacher involvement in curricular decisions as an important means for improving the quality of the teaching profession.

in the literature. Little was written in the effective schools literature about the place of teachers as policy makers. "Teacher efficacy," the capacity to instruct and get children to learn what one intends, was discussed, but not "teacher instrumentality." Reforms spawned by the publication of *A Nation At Risk* (The National Commission on Excellence in Education,1983) barely touched on the place of teachers in decision making in schools. A Carnegie Foundation study (1988) touted as the "most comprehensive [survey] ever conducted on the conditions of teaching" reported that "teachers are not sufficiently involved in making critical decisions," and are treated merely "as front row spectators in a reform movement in which the signals are being called by governors, legislators, state education officials—those who are far removed from the field of action." (p. 4) Although there has been some change since the Carnegie study, public school teachers still have little voice in education policymaking.

I sensed that there was something special about a school and its principal when teachers had a major voice in decision making. Typical school organization has been described (Abbott, 1969; Abbott & Caracheo, 1988; Bryk, Lee, & Smith, 1990; Hanson, 1991) as hierarchical, highly authoritarian, control oriented, inflexible, and forcing teachers to work isolated from peers and supervisors. Further, managers are characteristically inordinately powerful, both statutorily and implicitly and, typically, are seen as imperious toward teachers and support staff. Because school organization and managers tend to conspire against processes such as shared decision making, collaborative planning, and problem solving, I wanted to learn how and why these successful schools and their managers might be different.

I did not choose these schools under the assumption that only schools with high TPA are successful or good; clearly this is not true. Rather, my personal conviction that authority over one's work domain is a component of true professionalism, and the lack of literature examining that component of teachers' professional lives in successful or effective schools, simply led me to schools in which success or "good enoughness" and TPA coexisted.

Chapter 5

The Policy Environment

My intention to study the place and function of TPA in three success-ful high schools was not realized. During the early days of my first on-site stay, I sat in on a meeting at which faculty discussed length-ening the time students would study in a core curriculum. I realized teachers were using their professional authority in a collective, town meeting fashion, an approach quite different from what I had seen in other schools during site visits for the SSRP. One school had used a departmentally elected or appointed representative system; the other had also used a representative system, with schoolwide elections. I thought about this and recognized what I should have seen from the beginning: Teachers exercised TPA differently in different schools.

This recognition led me to queries that reshaped the study. I began to consider why TPA was exercised differently in one school compared to another. One possibility was that TPA was dif-ferent due to each school's unique history, student population and faculty, and community demographics—all of those inimitable context forces typically cited in explaining a school's uniqueness. This explanation could not be a mere possibility, of course; it had to be some of the cause, if not all of it.

I also considered the possibility that TPA differences related to and derived from other aspects of the schools. For example, I observed that TPA exercised though town meeting-like arrangements in one school was consistent with other aspects of that school. It had a community-like ambience and articulated an educational philosophy that invoked "community" in its expressed educational values, including egalitarian ideals and an emphasis on openness and belonging.

Another school's decentralized approach to administration fit the manner in which TPA was exercised; namely, TPA held sway primarily at the departmental level and through representative committees. Decisions were discussed and acted on within departments and passed on to schoolwide committees comprised of elected or appointed representatives from the departments. Departments at the second school served many of the communitarian functions served by the school community as a whole in the first.

Once I began to systematize variations in the expression of TPA at different schools, I saw that an answer to my question about the differences would most likely be found in the context of other dimensions of each school.

As I charted this new course and considered dimensions on which I would focus, I was influenced by the information I had already collected (e.g., role of the principal, purpose, climate), given SSRP's protocols and my own experiences and preferences. I was also influenced by the effective schools literature.

Because I was interested in building-level forces that moved professionals in these schools to work so hard, I looked to school policies: goal and mission statements, regulations governing teacher and student behavior, and policies that could be considered to motivate those in the school toward particular values or practices. I was interested in policy in its normative sense. I wanted to know the nature, place, and function of policy in explaining TPA, for example. By looking at dimensions such as TPA and tracing them back through policies that could be seen to "cause" or "create" these dimensions, I could begin to understand these dimensions as manifestations and results of policy.

POLICY AS NORMATIVE

Those who study "policy" agree generally that no single definition is universally accepted. Guba (1984) analyzed various conceptions of policy, each applicable in certain contexts and each an organizing principle for certain kinds of inquiries, data collection, and analysis.

Among the conceptions he examined were those that defined policy as:

- expressions of intents or goals
- accumulated decisions of a governing body to direct and influence matters in its purview
- a guide to discretionary action
- a strategy adopted to ameliorate or solve a problem
- formally and informally sanctioned behavior. (pp. 64-65)

Each of these conceptions points to or evokes authoritative principles, values, standards, guides, and rules for correct and binding behaviors. Simply put, each is normative. Policy is, then (or can be viewed as), a norm of conduct intended to consistently and regularly move an institution and those within it in particular valued directions. Policy in this normative sense served as an organizing principle for me as I undertook my study of dimensions of the schools.

My conception of policy for this study assumes that school characteristics can promote valued behaviors among students (and school professionals) independent of students' out-of-school experience. To believe otherwise would be to assume the view "schools do not make a difference." The effective schools research, limitations notwithstanding, has demonstrated otherwise; schools can and do make a difference. Metz's (1986) imaginative and cogent study comes to mind. Metz conducted a comparative study of two junior high schools in a city in which equal distribution of students by race and socioeconomic status was mandated by the school board. She found pronounced differences between the attitudes, conduct, and academic performance of the students in these schools. Given the comparable backgrounds of the students, she could convincingly conclude that differences were attributable to differences in the schools' characteristics. My assumption was thus strengthened by studies such as Metz's and those of other effective schools researchers (e.g., Brookover et al., 1982; Brookover & Lezotte, 1977; Rutter et al., 1979).

POLICY ELEMENTS

On-site observations, interviews, and examinations of documents led me to focus on dimensions of the schools that I thought would help me understand why TPA was exercised differently in each and why the schools functioned as they did. I collated the materials and information I was gathering relative to those dimensions that interested me and that seemed manifestly expressive of the essential character of the schools. Before I was far into classifying material from the first school, I found myself with categories such as "school purpose," "governance pattern," "teacher professional authority," "leadership," "school atmosphere," and "community respect for the school," among others. Each category subsumed a range of policy and policy-related information. Each policy datum, in turn, addressed or reflected one or another of the manifest dimensions that interested me or caught my attention as something that could not be ignored.

I debated what I might best call these categories of information that I was labeling as "school purpose," "leadership," and so on. "Dimensions" suggested itself first, but that term denoted little. I also considered "traits" and "characteristics" because my categories had all the earmarks of characteristics and traits. Of course they evoked the school success-school trait linkage of effective schools research.

However, the information I collected all related to policy. I was collecting and analyzing policies, and the traits I identified were policy based and inspired. The material did not merely demonstrate that each of these schools had, for example, a clear and compelling mission, or that principals exercised instructional as well as administrative leadership. It revealed the kind of mission, as well as whether it was clear, widely understood, shared, and compelling. And it explained the kind of leadership that was being exercised, by whom, and how. I was gathering materials that were about policy in a normative sense that was reflected in salient aspects of the schools that, in turn, were expressions and the ends of beliefs, values, and choices. They were the consequence of intentions that constituted policy and that were normative or directive.

For the reasons just explained, I arrived at the term *policy elements*: the salient policy-based and policy-inspired traits and processes that related to, were derived from, and were expressions of school building-level decisions that established principles, goals, rules, and strategies.

Policy element was not an immediately obvious unit of study. I came to it after realizing that what I had thought would be the unit— TPA—could not be understood except as one important aspect—element—of a much bigger picture involving other elements. Table 5.1 lists the policy elements that became the foci of my information collection and analysis. School mission, ambience, ethos, governance, organizational control, leadership, teacher professional authority, socialization, and moral authority were the policy-based and inspired dimensions—policy elements—that I focused on in my study. It is clear that my AHA! experience was premature.

Table 5.1. Policy Elements.

Labels and Definitions for Salient Policy-based Traits and Processes

MISSION:	*Ultimate Task and Fundamental Reason for Being*
AMBIENCE:	*Encompassing Atmosphere, Tone, and Feel*
ETHOS:	*Expressible Commonly Held Beliefs Invoked to Account for Policy, Behavior, and Operations*
GOVERNANCE:	*Dominant Mode of Policy and Decision Making and of Setting Goals and Direction*
ORGANIZATIONAL CONTROL:	*Dominant Mode of Enforcing and Regulating Behavior in Light of Policies, Goals, and Directions*
LEADERSHIP:	*Person or Group Who Functions as the Major Source of Influence Over Beliefs, Values, and Behaviors to Which Most Look for Overall Direction and Support*
TEACHER PROFESSIONAL AUTHORITY:	*Teacher Involvement and Importance in the Making of Institutional Philosophy, Goal Setting, and in Policy Making Generally*
SOCIALIZATION:	*Means of Inducting Newcomers and Making Their Beliefs, Values, and Behaviors Congruent with the Established Social System*
MORAL AUTHORITY:	*Capacity to Command the Respect of Significant Publics*

Once the domain of policy elements presented itself to me, it was obvious what some policy elements would be, given my experience with the schools, my early data bases and categories, and the influence of the school effectiveness research. School mission as a policy element derived from materials I collected regarding school purpose. I was interested in purpose in part because I had written with colleagues on the absence of purpose and the consequences of that void for public education (Raywid, Tesconi, & Warren, 1985). Further, effective schools research was clear regarding the essentiality of purpose for school effectiveness, and my initial site visits to these schools taught me a great deal about how important their missions were to them. Surely, then, the ways mission came about and functioned in each school, and how professionals in these schools saw their school mission, would be important.

Another obvious dimension was leadership. As with mission, I had collected a great deal of information regarding leadership because of the requirements of the SSRP and, again, because of the effective schools research. The latter was replete with studies of the principal's leadership and its place in school effectiveness. Such leadership, I was convinced, would play a role in influencing the place and prospects of teacher professional authority, and in helping to account for the nature and function of the school as well. I was convinced, moreover, that leadership in schools wherein teachers exercised a high degree of professional authority had to be different from leadership in schools with little or no TPA.

Governance and organizational control emerged as important policy elements, given my attention to leadership and policy matters in general. It seemed inappropriate to slight these matters in a study that spoke of policy elements and that necessarily considered matters of communication flow, division of labor, and regulatory and normative forces. They were surely important as policy elements in schools with a high degree of TPA. So these two elements presented themselves as salient and logical policy considerations worthy of special attention, given the unique governance and professional authority patterns in the schools.

The effective school literature had taught me a great deal about "climate" in schools, and my colleagues and I (Raywid, Tesconi, & Warren, 1985) had written about "user friendliness" as an aspect of school climate in successful schools. Also, my experience with the laid-off workers in Ruraldom suggested that a "loving" climate might be central for at least one high school. In short, I was predisposed to consider matters related to climate. Moreover, I could not have ignored it in any case. The character and feel of each school was palpable.

The climate in these schools was not accidental. Policy documents reflected the intentionality behind it and showed school professionals insisting on certain practices and rules to make the atmosphere what it was. Accordingly, I felt compelled to distinguish between atmosphere—hence, *ambience*—and the essential spirit or underlying ethic—hence, *ethos*—that might account for it. I chose to address ethos as a separate category and to use ambience instead of climate because the latter has come to be used in ways that blur what went into making school atmosphere what it is.

The moral authority of these schools was another policy element difficult to ignore. The influence each school exercised with the various segments of the public was impressive. Different groups listened to and deferred to each school in ways generally no longer seen nor expected. In subsequent chapters I describe how the moral authority of these schools was so strong that parents trusted school professionals and did not try to be involved in the operation of the school. Moreover, school professionals held authority over teaching and learning, sometimes absolving parents of responsibilities for tutoring, monitoring homework or attendance, or counseling and advising, that may have been beyond them.

Some policy elements were unexpected and emerged from my observations independent of convictions or expectations I held in advance. This was the case with TPA, for example, although I was impressed early in my contact with these schools by the high degree of TPA in each and how that contrasted with the literature. The research and related literature about teachers' place in decision making reflected a powerful consensus. Even in "effective" schools, teachers evidently had little to no voice in matters that shaped their schools. I did not expect to find TPA so salient.

Socialization was another element I did not anticipate. It was not obvious to me before seeing it that school professionals would respond to it so self-consciously, nor that the ways in which these schools socialized their new professionals would be so apparent. My reading of the effective schools and related literature had not left me sufficiently mindful of socialization to consider it a priori.

Some features I had thought would be important or salient policy elements turned out not to be. As I looked for some to which the effectiveness literature or my intuition pointed, I did not find nor could I document them. For example, if the research literature spoke with one voice relative to school effectiveness, it was in three areas: parental involvement, teacher efficacy (that is, classroom excellence), and leadership of the principal. From the beginning, then, I assumed that school-parent relations would loom large in my findings. That was not the case, however, at least not in the sense that I had expected.

I found little evidence that school-parent relations was important to the essential character of these schools. This is not to suggest that parents were unimportant in their childrens' success in these schools. This was outside the domain of my study. The point is that I simply did not find parental involvement of the sort discussed in the effective schools literature or in general rhetoric about schools, community, parents, and school performance.

Similarly, I did not find evidence of the salience of out-standing classroom teaching. I cannot report finding anything exceptional about the teaching I observed nor about how it was received. I expected otherwise. As I report in chapters to follow, I did find that professionals in these schools worked hard and col-laboratively at developing common approaches to instruction that reinforced one another's teaching. It was not the case, though, that classroom "stars" emerged, and there was no teacher frequently cited as influential in students' success. Again, this finding was a surprise.

A third domain that has been a focus of effective schools literature and thus the focus of countless inservice trainings (and even graduate school courses) is the area of the principal's lead-ership. I expected, given the wealth of information in this area, that principals would be visionary, charismatic, visible, strong leaders of instruction and of administration. It is not an indict-ment at all of the principals involved that in their particular highly successful schools none of them had all or even many of these highly touted characteristics. Each was important to the success of the school, but in ways different from those evoked by the effective schools literature.

POLICY ELEMENTS AS INTERRELATED

The policy elements of this study presented themselves early and often as interrelated and mutually supportive. This became increasingly evident as I considered relationships that existed among school professionals' educational beliefs and philosophy, school mission, TPA, governance, and policies and practices generally. When I came upon policies expressing something about mission or leadership, for example, I examined statements about educational philosophy to see if any relationship between these domains was expressed or implied. I looked at what if anything described relationships between mission and leadership, or between leadership and governance. When I considered statements of schoolwide purpose, or goals regarding content, learning, and curriculum, I checked them against other documents; for example, statements of educational philosophy, curriculum guides, course syllabi (when available), and lesson plans. I asked questions about apparent interrelationships in interviews I conducted.

Table 5.2 outlines sources from which each of the policy elements was derived. For example, in consideration of mission I looked to written statements about schoolwide and curricular and learning goals. I studied statements described as educational philosophy, and anything that seemed to express the institution's organizing and directional values, beliefs, and commitments. I checked curriculum guides, course syllabi, and lesson plans, and I asked questions of teachers, administrators, students, parents, school boards members, and others about each school's direction, purpose, and working structure.

It became clear to me that each policy element differed in nature and function in each of the three schools. Leadership, for example, was different in character and in function in each school. This variation was due to the decisions and the contexts that gave rise to the elements, as already suggested, to the configuration or pattern of salient policy elements, and to the interrelationships among policy elements. The context difference may have been due to unintentional forces as well. Original intents may have been lost to succeeding generations of staffs, or some policy elements may have been so long in evolution that intent was more a result than a cause. The latter circumstance would reflect the kind of policy that Guba (1984) called informal yet still normative because it had become "sanctified" over time.

THE POLICY ENVIRONMENT

Having identified policy elements, and having sources that led me to them, I concluded that the interrelationships among policy elements formed a pattern of connectedness worthy of note. I came to call this pattern a *policy environment*.

Policy environment refers to the aggregate of a school's

Table 5.2. Policy Elements and Their Sources.

MISSION: ULTIMATE TASK AND FUNDAMENTAL REASON FOR BEING . . .
                     AS REVEALED IN

—oral testimony/written statements of schoolwide goals
—oral testimony/written statements on curricular/learning goals
—oral testimony/written statements on educational philosophy
—curriculum guides, course syllabi, and lesson plans

AMBIENCE: ENCOMPASSING ATMOSPHERE, TONE AND FEEL . . .
                     AS REVEALED IN

—written statements of ideals about professional behavior
—oral testimony of professionals regarding job satisfaction
—expressions of concern for fellow professionals
—observed in-school interpersonal demeanor among professionals
—policies/observations regarding treatment of visitors
—testimony of parents and others about experiences as visitors
—professionals' observed behavior toward students
—external/internal appearance of school and testimony about same

ETHOS: EXPRESSIBLE COMMONLY HELD BELIEFS INVOKED TO
                     ACCOUNT FOR POLICY, BEHAVIOR, AND OPERATIONS . . .
                     AS REVEALED IN:

—school professionals' testimony regarding motivation
—testimony about commitment toward the school and its members
—values invoked to explain/justify decisions
—testimony regarding determinants of personal and school efficacy
—testimony regarding determinants of school's credibility

GOVERNANCE: DOMINANT MODE OF POLICY AND DECISION MAKING AND OF
                     SETTING GOALS AND DIRECTION . . .
                     AS REVEALED IN:

—standard rules and regulations
—nature, function, and composition of standing committees
—testimony/observations about the exercise of position power
—testimony/observations about place of formal/informal power
—division of labor relative to decision and policymaking

Table 5.2. Policy Elements and Their Sources (cont.).

ORGANIZATIONAL
CONTROL:
DOMINANT MODE OF ENFORCING AND REGULATING BEHAV-
IOR IN LIGHT OF POLICY, GOALS, AND DIRECTION . . .
AS REVEALED IN:

—testimony about the place of statutory and informal authority
—policy and testimony about sources and patterns of communications
—statutory/informal use of authority to allocate resources
—extent of delegation of authority and responsibility
—consensus on teaching and other professional practices

LEADERSHIP:
PERSON OR GROUP WHO FUNCTIONS AS THE MAJOR SOURCE
OF INFLUENCE OVER BELIEFS, VALUES, AND BEHAVIORS TO
WHICH MOST LOOK FOR OVERALL DIRECTION AND SUPPORT . . .
AS REVEALED IN:

—testimony/observation regarding exercise and sources of power
—testimony/observation about power over resource allocation
—policies/observation about sources of authority and control
—testimony/policies/observations about supervisory styles/aims
—decision and policymaking apparatus and processes

TEACHER
PROFESSIONAL
AUTHORITY:
TEACHER INVOLVEMENT AND IMPORTANCE IN THE MAKING
OF INSTITUTIONAL PHILOSOPHY, GOAL SETTING, AND IN
POLICYMAKING GENERALLY . . .
AS REVEALED IN:

—involvement in fashioning of educational philosophy
—establishing curricular, learning, and content goals
—textbook selection and evaluation
—curriculum design, development, and evaluation
—teacher, administrator, and support staff hiring and evaluation
—statutory documents, policy manuals, handbooks, minutes
—testimony of significant actors
—observations of policy and decision-making activities

SOCIALIZATION:
MEANS OF INDUCTING NEWCOMERS AND MAKING THEIR
BELIEFS, VALUES, AND BEHAVIORS CONGRUENT WITH THE
ESTABLISHED SOCIAL SYSTEM . . .
AS REVEALED IN:

—composition of hiring committees
—nature and function of teacher evaluation
—nature and function of supervisory processes
—existence, nature, and aims of mentoring practices
—testimony of significant actors about their experiences

Table 5.2. Policy Elements and Their Sources (cont.).

<u>MORAL</u> <u>AUTHORITY</u>:	CAPACITY TO COMMAND THE RESPECT OF SIGNIFICANT PUBLICS . . . *AS REVEALED IN*:

—testimony of significant actors
—documents shared with publics
—school promotional materials
—evidence cited in justifying school directions/actions
—press accounts of school
—written statements of educational philosophy
—written justifications for program/policy decisions

policy elements. Individually, considered independent of the overall policy environment, a policy element is a fragment of a school's being. Within a policy environment, however, each element is shaped by and, thus, to a greater or lesser extent is contingent on other elements with which it interacts.

For example, each school studied had a governance arrangement. Policies that created or reflected that governance arrangement also created and reflected TPA policies. The same was the case for the other policy elements.

The policy environment was normative, as was each policy element, but was far more powerful than individual elements. It was more than the sum of each school's parts.

SOME CONSIDERATIONS

Readers may see in "policy environment" some connection to school "culture." Studies of school culture follow popular studies of organizational culture in the business literature and in trade books. School culture, variously defined as "atmosphere" (Goodlad, 1984), "personality" (Tye, 1987), "ethos" (Rutter et al., 1979), "essence" (Lightfoot, 1983), "sharing of attitudes, beliefs, and values that bond disparate individuals into a community" (Grant, 1988), or "shared meaning system" (Metz, 1986), is typically conceived in broader and more complex ways than policy environment. It is broader than atmosphere, or ambience, or ethos as I use these two terms. "Culture" is even broader and more complex than some of the definitions of school "culture" suggest (see Page, 1990, and Schein, 1985).

"Policy environment" is distinct from school culture; it is more observable and less comprehensive. The culture of a school, then, would *subsume* the policy environment. However, for reasons I try to make clear in Part III, characterizations of school cultures are incomplete if they ignore policy environment.

Each policy environment described in the narratives and depicted in the policy environment Tables of Part II is made up of the nine policy elements presented in Table 5.1. The nine elements do not exhaust the elements that might exist in schools. They may not even represent the most salient of all policy elements that could be examined. They were identified as a function of the kind of data collected for this study because they captured my interest, or they appeared to converge logically to define a particular construct, or they reflected or refuted other effective schools findings. In the categorization that led to the nine policy elements, I looked for distinctions among policy elements, but I did not seek to name all possible elements.

The nature and function of the policy environment is discussed at length in Part III, following narratives about each school in Part II. It is noted now, however, that the policy environment perspective grounded in this study is presented as a foundation and framework for understanding a school. It is not the only one. It is certainly important, and perhaps necessary.[1]

The character of each school I studied is limned and revealed by policy elements which together form a policy environment that is unique. The study of effective schools and, more importantly, the mandating of school reform are less meaningful without attention to each school's policy environment and an understanding of the policy elements that give access to it.

---

[1]There are various ways to study humans in organizations. One approach, typically referred to as a *human resource approach*, focuses on human needs and the extent to which they are met in organizations; incentives and employee participation in the governance constitute some of the emphases in such approaches. *Symbolic approaches* emphasize ritual and symbolism, beliefs behind policies and practices, myths about organizations, and the meanings workers give to their work and their place in organizations. *Political approaches* tend to emphasize the nature and place of power and its distribution in organizations. *Structural approaches* stress the balance between certain kinds of controls, centralized versus decentralized features, the nature and function of communications systems and decision making, and the place of various actors and functionaries in the policy-making and decision-making apparatus of the organization. My study subsumes aspects of all of these approaches, a function of the fact that it was evolutionary, influenced by my site visitor role, the kinds of data and information it called on me to consider, and my false start with TPA.

Part II

The Schools and a Postscript

Overview

Each narrative to follow is preceded by an account of my impressions of the setting of each school, and then begins with a *Fact File*, an outline of statistical information relative to the school. These files are meant to be informative. They are not addressed directly or in detail in the narratives. The reader is invited to consider the implications of the statistics for each school and to refer back to them, given any questions and issues evoked by the narratives.

Extended descriptive accounts of the schools follow the Fact File. These narratives reflect the manner in which I was engaged by each school. Each moves back and forth from reportage to reflection, to analysis, or to commentary.

The substance and the manner of presentation reflect changes in my understanding of the school and its people as each visit progressed. They reveal my movement from being a stranger in each school, through increasing familiarity, to analyst and commentator. I have tried to recount how I experienced each school and have weaved my experiences into my reflections, analyses, and commentaries.

I have constructed the narratives so that what you read about each school addresses what I witnessed relative to the nine policy elements. As will be seen, these policy elements became both windows and halls of mirrors as I saw them, as well as data sources. People in the schools reflect themselves and each other in their magnificent process of creating places to teach and learn.

Chapter 6

Ruraldom Union High School

> *I've got two daughters at [Ruraldom], mister. It's a damn good school. I know. I'd have stayed in high school if mine was anything like it. And let me tell you, my girls are loved at that place, and they love it!*

The words of the father at the gas station were in my thoughts as I drove to Ruraldom Union High School.

Although the soothing, rolling hill terrain and evergreen lush mountains were appealing, the blight of decrepit housing and other structures outside the immediate vicinity of the school was pervasive. Trailers on the highway's edge were deteriorating. The yards around them were littered with broken down cars, bald tires, wheel-less bicycles. Shabbily dressed children and skinny dogs played in the rubble without visible adult supervision.

During my SSRP site visit, I had been told by school and social services personnel of inordinately high rates of all the social ills associated with poverty: clinical depression, abuse of alcohol and other drugs, and child and spousal abuse. For too many RUHS students this meant add-ons to the typical emotional baggage *of adolescence. School professionals at RUHS were reported to be especially sensitive and responsive to this reality.*

The school became visible as a small rise in the road gave way to a broad view of a valley hemmed on three sides by rolling hills and on the fourth by what was called a mountain in New England.

RUHS encompassed several acres in the valley and, except for some small buildings that served the paper industry, scattered trailers, and small bungalow houses, it was the only structure in the valley. The neatness of the setting and the athletic fields combined to make a bucolic picture that masked the economic and social blight elsewhere.

The exterior of the high school contrasted starkly with the signs of depression outside the shallow valley. The two story brick structure sat sprawled over well-tended grounds that included a football field, a track, a baseball diamond, and a soccer field. The playing fields were all well trimmed and marked.

I was soon to learn that the neat school grounds were matched by a clean and colorful interior that reinforced the welcoming atmosphere of the school. Walls were covered with posters, announcements, and murals. The floors shone. Everything was neatly arranged, reflecting a striking pride in the school's physical appearance. It all contrasted sharply with the signs of decline in the surrounding area. The contrast was so stark as to suggest the school as a haven, a refuge from blight and depression.

CASE #1: RURALDOM UNION HIGH SCHOOL

Fact File

Total number of students: **2 6 2**   Grades: **9 - 1 2**

Ethnic composition: **99% white, 1% Native American**

Percentage from low income families: **6 9 %**

Number of staff:

	Full-Time	Part-Time	Other
Administrators	1 Prin.	1 Asst Prin.	
Teachers	1 8	1	1FT Resource Rm Tch
Teacher Aides	3	0	1FT Migrant Ed Tch
Counselors	1	0	2PT Vol Tchr Aides
Library/Media Staff	1	0	1PT Psychologist
Social Workers	0	0	1PT School Tutor
Security Officers	0	0	
Food Service Staff	0	4	
Clerical Staff	2	0	

Percentage of professional staff with graduate degrees: **4 5 %**

Average length of service of professional staff: **1 1 years**

Organizational structure: **Departmental**

Selected outcomes of prior year's graduates[*]:
　　　enrolled in four-year college or university: **2 0 %**
　　　enrolled in a community college: **1 4 %**
　　　enrolled in vocational training: **1 0 %**
　　　employed full time: **1 0 %**
　　　employed part time: **1 0 %**
　　　enlisted in the military: **2 0 %**

Extracurricular participation rate: **8 9 %**

Drop-out rate: **3 %**

Average daily student attendance: **9 5 %**

Average daily teacher attendance: **9 8 %**

[*]The percentages do not add up to 100%, but were supplied by RUHS.

Ruraldom Union High School served about 260 students during the period of this study. Students came from three surrounding towns situated in a sparsely populated area of northern New England not far from the Canadian border. It had enrolled as many as 390 students, but that was before the demographics of the late 1970s and early 1980s brought a nationwide decline in students of high school age. It was also before the communities served by RUHS felt the consequences of other nationwide phenomena of the late 1970s and early 1980s: economic decline, high inflation, and recession. "Recession everywhere else maybe, but depression here," explained a school board member.

RUHS was a small high school, and some of its attractiveness and accomplishments were a function of its size. School professionals knew students and families well. They had the luxury of calling students' relatives about problems and knowing what to expect from them. The fact that in the school and in its communities everybody knew everybody helped to keep rambunctious adolescents in line. Even curricular matters could be changed or implemented quickly. The simple but important fact was that things got done because of familiarity and trust, due to the smallness of the school and of the communities served by it.

Many of Ruraldom's limitations and less attractive features were also due to size. These included lack of course and program offerings, lack of diversity, provincialism which limited students' horizons, limited opportunities for students with special needs or talents, and the necessity to serve many functions due to needs associated with poverty and limited community social services. When I asked a group of parents about the weaknesses of the school, the most common response spoke to curricular limits imposed by size and financial crisis.

"The fact that our school cannot offer a fourth year in a foreign language is a problem for some of our students. We don't have a course in advanced calculus. Such courses and much, much more are offered to students in high schools not too long a drive from us. But that is the way it is. We live with it knowing that the school people with so few resources are doing more than we have a right to ask."

Small size can be a blessing or a burden. At RUHS, it was both.

The three communities, comprised of about 2,500 residents, from which RUHS drew its students were all rural and, during the time span of this study, were struggling with a debilitating economic crisis. The wood harvesting, lumber, pulp, and paper industries on which these communities had relied and on which they had thrived were at a stand still, as the three angry men in the gas station made known to me. Income levels were low and declining; unemployment was high; welfare roles were crowded. Cultural experiences were minimal. Many families had chosen to leave the area in pursuit of better opportunities.

The student population of Ruraldom High School was reported to be 99% white; the remaining 1% was classified as Native American. A comparatively large Franco-American population was visible in the communities served by RUHS; French was the primary language of some townspeople. Proximity to Canada's province of Quebec accounted for this demographic feature, but the school's application form and associated documentation for the SSRP, as well as other school materials I collected, offered no reference to this population. The Franco-American population in some northern New England states was disproportionately represented among the poor and near-poor. No such association was claimed in information provided by school officials.

"Why," I asked the superintendent, "is there no attention to the cultural difference brought to school by the Franco-Americans? Couldn't that be a basis for some cultural educational opportunities?"

He indicated that such opportunity might exist elsewhere, but "not here. Our French speaking population has enough attention brought to it, given its high visibility among the poor and their social problems. They don't want their children or themselves singled out in school, and we try to honor that. I know that some think that we should take the lead and make this a positive thing, but we have other priorities and other problems."

A visit to a small grocery store with signs advertising "cold beer," "cigarettes," and "fishing licenses" was the beginning of my realization of the Franco-American presence. I stopped at this store frequently on my trip to and from the high school, and I talked with the woman who ran it, her children, who attended a nearby elementary school and, on occasion, to some of her customers. They all taught me a great deal about the area, the Franco-American influence in it, and about the high school.

Ruraldom has more than its share of poor. Sixty-nine percent of the students were reported as coming from low-income families, a figure based on the number of free and reduced-cost lunch applications. Although an acceptable means for determining a school's low-income population, the number of free and reduced-cost lunches was not always a reliable measure. In some communities there were more students on free or reduced lunch programs than census data or welfare roles warranted. In others, parents and students did all they could, in spite of sometimes abject poverty, to keep themselves off the free or reduced-cost lunch rolls to avoid the stigma that came with it; this was often the case in small towns. At Ruraldom, however, the reported rate appeared valid. The superintendent provided data on district-wide hot lunch eligibility, supported by census data. The percentage of low income students district-wide was 63% of the total school-system population.

Educators are accustomed to hearing the phrase, "I know good teaching when I see it, even if I cannot describe it." Similarly, I know when I am in a user-friendly school, even if I cannot describe it. The physical appearance of the building, the positive, welcoming spirit of the people in it, and the sense of pride that all took in it, made this school a very inviting place—for students, for members of the towns served, and for visitors.

"This school prides itself on its neatness and aliveness and looks like this all the time. We work at it," explained the assistant principal. "It is something we are self-conscious about. Don't you remember? It was like this when you visited for the Recognition Program." He was correct, as my original notes confirmed. The place looked as new as it had two years earlier, even though it had been built in the late 1950s.

"Do you think we could afford to manicure the outside grounds and fix the building simply for a visitor?" asked the guidance counselor. "The inside maybe, if we were so inclined, but in no way could we give a hurry-up fix to the outside."

A teacher noted that students had been encouraged to paint the interior walls with various scenes and cartoons to "make them look less institutional than most school hallways. It's also a way of displaying and rewarding talent among our kids and of getting them to have some ownership in keeping this place nice."

Another teacher said, "students are expected to contribute to the cleanliness of the building and grounds. Students seen messing up hear about it from others—students and teachers. And if we see somebody doing something good, we praise them."

I learned later that the school put together teams of volunteers—students, teachers, and other school staff—to work for a month in August before school opened, and in March and April to help the custodian with the grounds and other upkeep. "We can't afford custodians to do all the jobs that must be done. So, we involve the school community in it," the principal told me. "We are maintaining the place when otherwise we would not be able to, and we are teaching kids something about keeping their own nest clean."

In another conversation the principal again brought up this matter of all joining in to keep up physical appearances. "I believe whatever your conditions, and ours are absolutely dollar poor, the resources are around you. You have to look for them in people and figure out how to use them. It's willingness to do a lot of work and it's pushing people to chip in."

Faculty, students, and community members spoke of the school in intimate and possessive ways. Terms like "family" and "our school" were used frequently when explaining it to outsiders. The principal settled on "family" when searching for the one dimension of the school that captured its essence. He also used it and "community" when functioning ceremonially with the faculty or student body in celebrating some individual or group achievement, or when he was extolling the benefits of membership in RUHS. There can be a cloying, artificial character to these terms, but I did not feel that when I heard them used at Ruraldom.

"You've been around enough and seen enough here to know that we have some serious problems," a board member exclaimed to me following some of my questions about RUHS, specifically about the pride people have in it. "We stay up here for all kinds of reasons. It's cold, parts of the area are in bad shape, and with some of the rotting cars and other junk all around it looks pretty bad. But if you like space, if you like fishing and hunting, if you like your kids to have a sense of freedom to roam without adults looking over them all the time, then this place has something for you. And the school is a good reason to stay. I know that my kid couldn't get more out of his high school years than he got out of this school. With all our shortcomings, it's the best."

Teachers referred to most of their colleagues as "friends" and sometimes as "teammates" enrolled in a common cause: "To give these kids a chance to better their lives," as a science teacher put it. "That is what our job is really all about."

A history teacher observed that teachers and the principal worked at generating the upbeat, inviting community atmosphere and at embracing everybody connected with the school. He explained that "a feeling of warmth and friendliness fills the school. I think it's due to a mutual trust and respect among students, faculty, and administration. We created this kind of climate by meeting one another's needs, which takes time and patience. This climate fosters the feeling that students are respected, and that inspires them to work to achieve the best they can. And it helps us to keep alive on the job and excited in our work."

A science teacher commented that "more of us have worked together on school business than I ever thought possible. Just about all of us meet together often, work together, and share ideas and complaints. I like coming here every day." Another teacher expressed similar sentiments: "The climate nurtures the total person, whether students or teachers. We consider how can we help our community, our students, our school grow together, improve how we see one another. We concentrate on what will help all of us change for the better."

Some teachers referred to the students as "raw material" for whom RUHS was at once a kind of manufacturing plant and an oasis. "We work with what they bring and commit to educate and train them," observed an English teacher. "Our aim is to give them a better chance than what their parents had, although in some cases the parents had better chances than these kids would, were they going to another school."

Another teacher observed that the school "should be a shelter or a haven for the kids. They don't have it very easy these days. I'm glad I don't have to grow up in these times. On top of all the difficulties of being a teenager in this day and age, these kids have to deal with all kinds of bad stuff at home. We have a responsibility to do what we can to make their lives better than what they see around them."

For all those school professionals who accepted it in all its ways, RUHS was a place they loved. There were, though, a few who did not fit. One of the marginal teachers who had been at RUHS three years remarked, "I could not and would not adjust. I don't think the uniformity demanded of teachers is healthy or wise educationally. So I don't fit. I know it, and others for sure do. If I had options I wouldn't be here now."

Students spoke of their teachers as "friends" and "confidants," and as like "fathers," "mothers," "sisters," and "brothers" when speaking of teacher-student relations. They reported receiving "a lot of attention and recognition" and of "getting support from the principal."

The guidance counselor pointed out that this school "really likes to play the in loco parentis role. In some cases we have to and in others we sort of relish it. High schools now are trying to avoid it."

One Ruraldom parent, accompanied with the nodding approval of others, observed that "respect, appreciation for teachers, and love for one another sum up what the school is all about." Another, evoking the finger-poking man in the gas station, remarked that "we would have loved to go to a school like this."

A middle-aged teacher, experienced in several other school systems, reported that his comparatively long tenure at Ruraldom "is unusual for me. I have always liked going to and living in different places. This is my eighth year, and that is a lot of time in one place for me. The rapport among teaching staff and between them and the administration and the community is the best and most comforting I have ever experienced. I feel secure here. Safe. It was the best decision I ever made to come here. I found teachers helping teachers. I am treated as a professional and as a special human being here. It's too comfortable for me to move."

The community-like ambience of Ruraldom High was no accident. It may originally have been a function of serendipity, not an easy matter to track down. Now a community spirit was cultivated. School professionals consciously made rules and regulations to create community in the school. Faculty meetings, conducted like New England town meetings, often included references to activities, new and long extant, that maintained the climate. A student handbook addressed the pride school professionals, parents, and former students took in the user-friendly character of the school, and admonished students to contribute to it. The principal noted that making the institution "less institutional" was an early aim of his. By the time of my visit, everybody was as invested in keeping it up as he was in establishing it seven years earlier.

The intentional character of this ambience was, in part, a function of an ethos that emphasized effort on behalf of the "common good." Symbols of community ties, such as dress codes, emblems, songs, posters, and art work on the walls were created to communicate to those in and outside the school (especially to those inside) that Ruraldom was a special place—a community committed to enhancing the life chances of its charges. Teachers and parents, in seeking to communicate this specialness, reported that people who graduated years ago came back for visits. A senior girl said that RUHS would not be an easy place to leave. "I hope I haven't become too dependent on the school. I guess I'll find out when I go the [State University]."

Organizational forums, such as school business meetings conducted like town meetings, were open to students and to all school personnel. Administrator and teacher open-door arrangements, multiple lines of communication, and school committees made up of students, faculty, administrators, parents, and nonprofessional staff all reflected the effort to build and maintain community. Twice a year, meetings of parents, students, and all school professionals were held to consider new ideas to make the school an even better place for its users.

Rules and regulations to ensure community were created and constantly fine-tuned. Behavior codes for Ruraldom students on and off campus, and ritualized events such as pep rallies, assemblies, field days, meditation breaks (when students and teachers reflected quietly on their own place and prospects in RUHS), award ceremonies, Boosters rallies, and required school-wide participation in day-opening and closing activities—all these were in service of the same goals: to build, to communicate, and to maintain a community spirit. Special activities such as school-community potluck breakfasts, retreats, schoolwide entrepreneurial enterprises, field trips, and community service further helped to bind people to the school and to those in it. They also served to distinguish the school from others. Some teachers visiting RUHS for an inter-scholastic athletic meet spoke with a touch of envy about what they perceived as the "pulling together" of the people associated with Ruraldom.

My first Wednesday in this school brought a first-hand encounter with one of these special activities. I arrived at the school quite early, a little after seven o'clock, on an early Fall morning. I had made up my mind to often show up early to see the start-up of a day, to observe students as they got off buses or out of their cars, and as they walked and talked their way into the cafeteria or their homerooms. I hoped to get a sense of what student mood, behavior, conversations, and the like might reveal about the school at the beginning of a day.

As I approached the school, I was surprised to see that the parking lot was overflowing with cars. It was too early for students to be on campus, so I assumed that the principal had arranged some kind of special assembly to introduce me; he had mentioned the possibility in a telephone conversation before I arrived. Consequently, I was taken aback when I walked into the school and no one was there to greet me.

I walked down a few halls, peeked in a few doors, and finally found my way by following the noise. I looked into an overflowing cafeteria. It was crowded with people of all ages, infants to senior citizens. Eventually I was approached.

"Are you our researcher-in-residence?" I was asked by a smiling woman. "Welcome. I'm Lia Wright [not her real name], the guidance counselor. Could I get you some coffee?"

"I'd love some coffee, thank you. What's going on?"

"Oh, this is Wednesday. Our weekly potluck breakfast."

I soon learned that the potluck breakfast was one of several activities, certainly the most successful by the indicator of attendance, aimed at maintaining goodwill between the school and the communities served.

Some other community-building and maintenance activities were equally impressive and telling. In the midst of a rural, economically depressed area, RUHS hosted between 400 and 500 adult education students per semester out of a total adult population of about 2,500. These extraordinary numbers were, again, no accident. Classes were offered during the day as well as in the evening, sometimes enrolling several generations of students. Parents and occasionally grandparents were in the same day or evening class with their children and grandchildren. This alone required policy and other kinds of machinations typically absent in American high schools. The aim of all these was not merely to ensure good enrollments. It served the community and added to other efforts to build and maintain community within the school and between the school and its publics. The school also served as a center for civic meetings.

All these served to sustain the belief central to this school's way of being: that Ruraldom was unique, that it was better than other schools, and that it served as a countervailing force to real and perceived negative external forces. All the bond building, nurturing, and maintenance efforts reflected a chosen and burdensome creation of responsibility to a school that was a supportive, empowering community. This feature of RUHS was reflected in other aspects of the school. Even a cursory reading of the elements of Ruraldom's policy environment in Table 6.1 reveals the pervasiveness of this ambience. Put another way, all the elements reflected beliefs, values, behaviors, and courses of action inclined toward community. "Inclusiveness is what motivates much that we do," said a history teacher, "and caring for everyone makes it possible."

The community ambience and common-good ethos was palpable to me as it reportedly was to nearly every one who visited Ruraldom. As one teacher put it: "A very healthy climate exists here. The art work throughout the building provides a great, agreeable atmosphere. A visitor to this place cannot but be impressed with the warm feel of it, from the appearance of the building and the polite students and their behavior to the way school staff treat you. You leave here with good feelings, and that's the way we want it."

Another teacher commented that "the open policy and the

Table 6.1. The Policy Environment of Ruraldom Union High School.

MISSION:	*To provide social, emotional, and academic support in order for students to be invested and successful in achieving their potential in various of life's domains.*
AMBIENCE:	*A community-like, collegial, cooperative, and user-friendly atmosphere; a positive and upbeat demeanor to the physical plant and to the way all greet and treat one another and visitors.*
ETHOS:	*Civitas, egalitarianism, unity, and stability capture an esprit generated from an ethic of caring and working for others and the school.*
GOVERNANCE:	*Collaborative, collegial, and organic; "town" meetings for discussion, policy-making, and decision are favored; all members of the school community have some say in some things.*
ORGANIZATIONAL CONTROL:	*Control is exercised informally, horizontally, and for uniformity. It arises from custom and the collective. De facto authority rules, whereas de jure authority is tolerated. All appears a function of negotiated order.*
LEADERSHIP:	*Principal, first among equals, is empowering, nurturing, and relationship oriented. Authority and responsibility are delegated, and leadership is exercised by teachers.*
TEACHER PROFESSIONAL AUTHORITY	*Covers many policy and program matters. It is exercised in a collective manner and is central to the school's character and operations.*
SOCIALIZATION:	*Self-consciously implemented, ensuring that newcomers feel strongly pressured to adopts school's philosophy and style. The main goal is to socialize all to be in and of the school, to maintain the existing social order.*
MORAL AUTHORITY:	*Success and efficacy generate praise, respect, strong support, and deference from the school's publics. Parents are freed from some typical expectations. School professionals act and are treated as such.*

limited open design of the building give access to students who need academic assistance, and encourage personal interaction with teachers and administrators. Students work together, tutoring or in study groups, to attain their goals. Face it, this part of the state is not the ideal, and with all the social problems around here, these kids need a place where they can feel good. Sometimes, we need it, too."

The community ambience, the sense of belonging and caring—again, these were not accidents. The ambience was known to teachers, administrators, and students; they extended themselves to tell visitors about it, and they referred to it in their self-studies and in their written and oral statements of belief and philosophy.

The planfulness of this ambience was also reflected in policy manuals, handbooks, minutes of faculty meetings, and other school documents. It was addressed in discussions and decisions reported in minutes of meetings, in handbooks, and in memoranda from the principal. I witnessed what teachers called "in-house workshops" at which some of these community-building initiatives were started and fleshed-out. They were held frequently. At the end of classes, school professionals discussed problems and proposed solutions or strategies.

One teacher, obviously speaking for the others in the room, said, "Three things account for our success. There is a positive interaction between school personnel and students that we are consistently working on. We are always reviewing where we have been, where we are, and where we are going. And, we have a comprehensive approach throughout the school to accent what we do well and to continue to improve." The principal pointed out that several initiatives taken during the past few years had helped "to make us a better school. We have implemented joint student, teacher, administrator planning. A comprehensive student survey led to many changes we incorporated prior to school opening. We constantly refer to the data from that survey to change and adjust to student needs."

Ruraldom as it existed was constructed by these people. "Teaching in this country is one of the loneliest professions," explained one of the math teachers. "It rewards the independent, loner type, the good and the bad one equally. Physicians consult with other physicians all the time. All the professions do. Not teachers. Most just tough it out. No wonder so many seem a bit different if not 'wacko'. Not here. We work together all the time to do our jobs and to make this place better."

Among all the groups interviewed, from students to school board members, individuals reported that they or others from

their groups had a hand in shaping purpose and mission statements. Such statements, they agreed, were routinely brought
before parent and community groups and returned to the school
professionals for final review and action. Several teachers, students, and parents agreed that an in-place process at the department level led to the selection of goals and objectives that became
bases for similar processes schoolwide. "We wanted our mission
to be known, generally supported, and owned by as many as possible," reported the principal. That mission as expressed in various written documents is:

> To provide a curriculum, formal instruction, a climate, an
> esprit, and models of humanness that demonstrate concern
> for the well-being of all in [RUHS] and that inspire and sup-
> port students to explore every opportunity and accept chal-
> lenges to fulfill their potentials and their aspirations.

I asked several people in the school if this mission was
developed and then used to create the ethos, ambience, and other
clearly chosen aspects of the school's character. All agreed this
was not the case. The principal noted, "I don't think I had the time
or will to invest in trying to settle upon mission. Settling upon a
purpose that is taken seriously in all you do takes a very long
time and is a hard struggle. I tackled how we felt about ourselves
and each other first, with teachers and students. You've got to have
all aspects of the community join in the creation of a mission."

Representatives of all significant actor groups could
articulate Ruraldom's mission; they did so in ways that reflected
congruency with written statements. Handbooks, policy manuals,
and curricular documents that touched on mission also did so in
ways congruent with what was understood by all significant
actors' groups.

Pride in having participated in the establishment and justi-
fication of the school's mission was evidenced in testimony from all
constituents. One parent said he knew he was speaking for others
when he observed that the widespread criticisms of public schools
that were popular at the time did not apply to Ruraldom. "Let the
people who think schools are in bad shape come here," he said, "to
see what a good high school looks like and how it got that way."

This shared understanding, widespread sense of ownership, and pride of place served to affirm and strengthen community. Policy documents and practice called for the involvement of
the various groups in fashioning the school's mission. Shared

understanding and ownership of the school's fundamental reason for being were, then, not accidents.

The overall mission of RUHS reflected the consciously created ambience and ethos of the school. Mission was expressed in broad social forms. To be sure, academic, intellectual, and vocational-technical pursuits were valued and honored in this school. Indeed, the college-bound rate relative to the socioeconomic composition of the student body suggested that academic achievement was the most important purpose. The percentage of disadvantaged students who went on to two-year or four-year colleges made this place extraordinary. A statewide report ranked RUHS 10th and 11th among the state's high schools for college-bound rates the two years immediately prior to my time there. This was a remarkable performance. The statewide ranking included schools serving some of the wealthiest communities in the northeast. "We have sent 65% of the students to some form of college training more often than not in the recent past," reported the principal. "Poor economics are making things even worse. So our rates these days do not tell the full and real story."

The principal and others insisted that academic successes were maintained because Ruraldom's students perceived faculty and staff as caring, supportive, and trustworthy. These school professionals justified their choice of a community-like nurturing mission in light of the socioeconomic condition of the students, the limited and limiting economic and cultural opportunities from which they came, and the individual and collective futures these limits would portend without systemic support. They felt compelled to convince students that RUHS offered a haven and an opportunity.

> Commit yourself to [RUHS] if you agree to be a member of its community [admonished a letter from the faculty to students], and you will come to realize that you will be cared for, supported, and given opportunities for achievements that you might not have thought possible. . . . We must all work together and for one another. If everybody works together for the common good, the individual benefits as well.

Some noteworthy examples of the commitments this choice evoked further illuminated the extra caring and supportive ethic of this school and its staff. Consider that this school had just one guidance counselor. However, college and career counseling were integrated into the school's program of student development. In fact, the counselor and other support staff, including cafeteria and custodial staff, described themselves as fully integrated into the day-to-day business of the school. They rejected the typical view that support staff members, professional or otherwise, were merely delivering a service on demand. "We think," reported the guidance counselor, "that having counselors teach courses or parts of them takes advantage of their skills and knowledge in the classroom. Same with librarians and others. Even our cooks are brought into some of our classes to talk about health and safety, and sometimes about chemistry and math."

The guiding assumption of the college and career counseling initiatives was that students who felt good about themselves had the resources to succeed in school, in college, and in life, their social and economic situations notwithstanding. Student response to this value, best reflected in drop-out, college-bound, employment, and military enlistment rates, suggested that students did indeed come to believe in themselves and their futures. Despite the lack of dollar resources, Ruraldom had developed several practices that worked effectively toward heightening of student life chances. Some involved college and career counseling and included:

- financial workshops conducted by admissions and financial aid officers from colleges and universities within the state
- a portrait gallery of photographs taken on college visits (to offset difficulties of taking all students directly)
- a career explorations unit as part of the English classes for junior and senior vocational students
- initiatives resulting in the waiver of some college application fees for low income students
- exposure to college possibilities through fairs and visits to as many campuses as possible
- use of computer software programs and networking opportunities to ensure student access to as much guidance information as possible
- a community-wide conference on raising aspirations ("Goal Boosters Conference")
- one-on-one meetings by the guidance counselor with each student in the high school
- a community-driven scholarship fund to help fund college attendance that raised $10,000 the prior year
- opportunities for "job-shadowing" in the surrounding

communities that helped set student sights on future possibilities
- continual use of counselor and teacher networks beyond Ruraldom to encourage contacts with students, to reinforce staff encouragements, and to help raise student aspirations

Another example of reaching out that made real the statements of the mission was the school's special emphasis on extracurricular activities. RUHS professionals and staff were convinced that extracurricular activities were important means for teaching students about their strengths and for keeping them engaged in the life of the school. An "extra legal" requirement obligated all students to participate in at least one extracurricular activity. "We believe," said one teacher, "that extracurricular activities can be a fun part of school, and that we must go out of our way to make sure that all get a chance to have fun in school. This is especially important for those kids who might drop out. Extracurricular stuff can be the hook to keep them in."

Teachers, staff, and other students worked mightily to arrange car pools to accommodate students who could not arrange transportation. An extensive intramural schedule of volleyball, basketball, and other athletic programs was designed to attract even the most recalcitrant of students. As in other arenas, teachers and others at RUHS worked extraordinarily hard to improve the life chances of these students.

My early morning starts made for some long days, especially when the days ended with attendance at some evening function or interview session. One very long day was occasioned by my attendance at some evening classes. Students with special family or related obligations were allowed to take courses in the evening school, if those courses were the same as those offered during the day. Sometimes students took these courses with their parents or other relatives.

I learned that farming responsibilities or helping out with family tree-harvesting enterprises were the obligations that precluded daytime school attendance. There were only about 10 students involved.

Night classes were a satisfying accommodation for all concerned. They were another piece of evidence that school authorities were willing to extend themselves to ensure that their students remained in school.

At about 10:00 pm the night class ended, and I returned to

the library where I had been given work space. There I saw a teacher who had been at the school since 7:30 that morning.

"I'm waiting for some girls," she responded to my surprised query. "They were rehearsing a skit for the class competitions. I direct the skit and give the girls rides home. The activity bus is long gone."

"Do you have far to take them?"

"I'll get home close to midnight."

The consequence of all this adult involvement was an exceptionally high extracurricular activity rate of about 89%. "We are absolutely convinced," said the counselor, "that our low dropout rate in the face of so much poverty is partly due to this." Perhaps the relatively high college-bound rate was also explained, at least in part, in this way. "Perhaps it was the caring in all this," said a welfare parent whose daughter would be entering a state college next year. "I can't imagine my girl getting this chance at another high school."

The school's approach to serving all students' interests and needs and to reaching out in ways evoked by the mission statement was reflected in other unusual and imaginative ways. For example, school resources did not permit the regular offering of art courses, much less a regular art curriculum. But student interest was generated and student need addressed by what the principal described as "initiatives to give talent an opportunity for expression." One such initiative was evidenced by the already mentioned art work on walls throughout the entire building. "Students are encouraged to contribute art work to these displays and to participate in local and state sponsored competitions," said the principal. "Approximately 10 students per year do so," he reported. One teacher noted how the display of student art contributed to the positive school climate. "It gives students a chance to show their work and to make this place look and feel good." In addition, art courses were offered occasionally in evening school as interest and demand dictated, and interested students were encouraged to enroll for credit.

Recognition of quality student performance—academic or otherwise—was valued at RUHS, and school professionals worked hard to ensure that as many students as possible got some kind of recognition. At the end of every month, all teachers selected a student from one of their classes for a "Classroom Student-of-the-Month Award." Students were selected for responsible behavior, attendance, cooperation, willingness to try new assignments in the subject, willingness to be helpful to other students or teachers, and willingness to have school work displayed. Selected students were written up for publication in the school and local newspapers, sometimes with photographs. These write-ups plus a group photograph of all those selected each month were posted outside the principal's office.

In addition to this, there were other awards that recognized student performance. For example, at the end of each marking period, teachers were asked to recognize students from all grade levels who were infrequently recognized, although their academic and other performance suggested that perhaps they were overlooked. The result was that many students received recognition of some sort. "We believe," reported the guidance counselor, "that just about everybody is worthy of some recognition for something or other."

The effort to reach out reflected and contributed to the school's ethos, which demanded that civitas—the common good—be supreme. This ethos was also reflected in some seemingly mundane ways. A "BIG E" (for "effort") board displayed in the main hallway recognized weekly those "tryers" and "hard-workers" selected by teachers. The "I OWE YOU ONE" board, also displayed in the main hallway, contained student and teacher expressions of gratitude, or simply general acknowledgements of those who had contributed to the well-being of the school or someone in it.

The strong sense of shared purpose, undergirded by shared belief and value systems, made Ruraldom a potent and directive social and moral force in the lives of its students. Both the directiveness and the potency of the school were visible in a uniformity of experience in domains of academic standards, behavior, participation, and student-teacher relations.

Schools lacking a directive and shared sense of purpose have been described as fragmented and have been seen as serving as mere neutral settings without moral force or direction (Powell, Farrar, & Cohen, 1986). RUHS served as a clear contrast. Students listened to this school's professionals; they trusted them and worked hard to satisfy them. The community trusted the school professionals and tended to let them run the school untethered by constraints often found in small towns and rural communities.

There is a lesson here. Moral authority comes from hard work, from professional dedication that far outsteps minimum performance standards, and from shared commitment.

Because Ruraldom's teachers were committed to schoolwide planning, development, and policy and decision making, it was no surprise that teacher talk indicated their primary loyalties were not to disciplines, not to some abstract notion of student needs, not to departments, not even to the profession, but to the institution.

Orientation and related activities that were in place were aimed at maintaining Ruraldom's ambience and valuing of the community over the individual. Supervisors believed it was important to help teachers reconcile their beliefs, values, personalities, and teaching styles to the philosophy and direction of the school. "We make it clear what we expect," reported one veteran teacher. "Those who do not like it here, who cannot work under this system, fine, we do not condemn. We know that this is not for everyone, and they can leave."

If misfits could not or would not submit to Ruraldom's ethos, they were pushed to marginality very quickly. According to the principal, "most teachers and administrators are taught that individual styles and philosophy should be strengthened in a school. We believe that can create chaos and lead to no system."

There were only two "out of sync" teachers I met at Ruraldom. One told how her commitment, her way of teaching and maintaining discipline did not match what her department wanted. "After two years, I find myself being ignored at meetings. The supervisor used to visit my classes about once a week. She's never there now."

I asked others about this teacher's isolation and its causes. No one responded in a mean-spirited way, but neither was anyone apologetic. The overwhelming majority of people connected with the school had chosen to conform in pursuit of shared goals. Those that did not conform were not allowed to get in the way. They were in essence shunned.

"I know that everyone thinks very highly of this school," exclaimed the other "outsider." "I do not think that conformity is good for anybody. A great deal of creativity and imagination are being lost. And families of school professionals are breaking up because the school is supposed to come before everything else. I will get out as soon as I can. But I will be whole and so will my marriage and family."

Teachers and supervisory personnel in noncommunity-like schools express values and beliefs different from Ruraldom's and more like those of this isolate teacher. They think it is important, for example, to ensure that teachers employ autonomy and discretionary authority. They value and encourage diverse personalities and styles. Indeed, this cultivation of pluralism of personalities and styles constitutes what is attractive about such schools to the professionals in them. It is what is taught to in-place and aspiring school professionals in schools of education and professional development programs throughout this country.

At Ruraldom, however, frequent, informal, and formative teacher evaluations reflected an "accept our perspective, be con-verted if need be, move on and out if unable" approach. Formal teacher evaluations that were mandated by negotiated contracts were honored and conducted according to schedule and policy, but treated in a pro forma manner. Informal evaluation went on con-tinually and moved teachers to perform in a manner consistent with, as one teacher put it, "[Ruraldom's] way of life."

"We feel we are number one," said one teacher as his peers nodded agreement, "[and] we take pride in that. We want to stay number one. That means making sure that each of us helps contribute to a [Ruraldom] impact on these students and towns. That means creating a system, a team of reinforcers, not everyone doing his own thing."

The reinforcement included recognition by all concerned of teacher performance. Among such recognition was a "teacher of the month" award started by the Student Council. All students, teachers, administrators, staff, parents, or others were invited to nominate teachers for this award. The Student Council selected the teachers from among all nominees, and the award was a certificate presented along with other awards at a monthly assembly. The teacher was written up by the Student Council and that report along with the teacher's photograph was printed in the school and local newspapers and posted outside the principal's office with other recognitions.

As faculty socialization was not left to chance, neither was the socialization of students. A student survey was conducted three times a year by the Student Council. The survey sought students' views on a variety of school policy matters, as well as their plans and interests regarding courses. "We work very hard to make sure that true student interests and views get reflected in what we do," observed the guidance counselor. "This survey has become very important for students. It is a way of showing them that we take them seriously."

The student survey reflected the extraordinary efforts to serve students, to get them "hooked" on RUHS and its way. Teachers and staff acknowledged this; it was also the case with rules and regulations. All agreed that rules for behavior at Ruraldom were well known, punishment for infractions was clear and known, and the meting out of penalties was fair. One teacher reported: "Our emphasis is on what needs of the student might account for misbehavior. We try to find out what those needs are early, so that we can anticipate and head off rule breaking."

Another teacher indicated: "We see students as mature persons and we stress their accomplishments. We play down the negatives. Praise stimulates a further striving for excellence."

Organizational arrangements at Ruraldom reflected a governance structure and practice commensurate with the community ambience and the "common good" ethos. Governance was communal, that is, it was horizontal, decompartmentalized, and congruent with an authority pattern that arose from the group based on custom and tradition. These patterns were also congruent with an atypical (Lou Harris & Associates, 1985) degree of teacher professional authority.[1]

I observed teachers' positions and functions on standing and ad hoc committees, on task forces, and in official general, departmental, or program faculty meetings wherein the following constituted the raison d'etre for the committee, task force, and/or meeting:

- strategic and long-range schoolwide planning
- content and schoolwide learning goals
- curricular design, development, and/or evaluation
- discipline and attendance policy
- textbook selection and evaluation
- peer and staff evaluation and development
- teacher reward and incentive programs
- teacher opportunities for advanced study
- education policy generally

The intent here was to witness the place and functioning of teachers in arenas and relative to matters that shape the policy environment in which they must perform, the goals they must pursue, the means they must employ in pursuit of those goals, and the norms and beliefs that determine the wisdom, value, and effi-

---

[1]The Metropolitan Life Poll of the American Teacher conducted by Lou Harris and Associates showed that reform initiatives had been implemented without input—much less a decisive voice—from teachers. Sixty-three percent of teachers said they had never been consulted and could not identify who had been consulted regarding school reforms. According to Harris, results like these suggested that a serious mistake has been made. Forty-one percent of the teachers polled by Harris wanted out of teaching because they lacked a voice in the shaping of the policy environment within which they had to pursue others' goals.

cacy of all these. Teachers, administrators, and school board members were interviewed in order to solicit their reactions to the findings of the observations and to establish their views on the place of teacher professional authority in their school's success and relative to teacher status.

Teachers in Ruraldom exercised a degree of professional authority not typically found in American high schools. Teachers at RUHS:

- fashioned schoolwide content, learning, and curricular goals
- shaped various schoolwide long range and strategic planning and development initiatives
- exercised an authoritative voice in schoolwide curricular polices
- strongly influenced the selection and evaluation of textbooks, peers, and staff
- exercised a major voice in the nature and direction of school-community affairs

In short, teachers manifested a degree of authority relative to their policy environment not generally found among secondary school faculties. "We all work in trust and cooperation, share responsibility for and own what goes on in this place," stated the principal.

I asked the principal if he thought the high TPA detracted from classroom teaching. "I know that our teachers are very, very busy because of their committee assignments. And I know they get tired. So I suppose in that sense the answer to your question is yes. However, these teachers, and I, too, think that wider responsibilities are part of their professional roles. They have to become involved as leaders, as mentors, as administrators in some ways. When you have all these responsibilities spread out among all the teachers and staff, you get a better sense of responsibility from everyone. Teachers see, and everyone sees that schoolwide rules and schoolwide business affect what happens in their shops."

The high degree of TPA at RUHS and the value accorded it did not derive from contractual or union obligations and power. They arose from acknowledgement among teachers, administrators, and board members of the importance of teachers in making the educational enterprise. TPA of this sort is not to be confused with the kind of teacher authority typically suggested by the term "teacher autonomy." This term refers principally to the statutory and discretionary authority teachers enjoy as supervisors of classrooms, and as they function in isolation from and independent of other adults, peers, or supervisors. Indeed, the sometimes jealous protection of autonomy would erode bases of shared governance and collaborative planning so important to the unique TPA of Ruraldom.

The important overall finding in Ruraldom relative to TPA and other traits and processes was that it was only one of many social system, organizational, policy, and cultural dimensions that made up and characterized the school. Combined, all these facets and more added up to a reality unique to each school, in this case to the *policy environment* of a "good enough" high school.

The principal at Ruraldom was important because of who he was, more than because of his position. One-way directives were seldom used. Multiple interactions were typical. Leadership by authority derived from position in a power echelon, so typical of American high schools, was replaced here by leadership that was shared, group-endorsed, and based on knowledge. Decision making was spread out.

To use the principal's words, "I see myself, and I think others here do, too, as a facilitator. I try to involve everybody in creating a community. Community, I think, is the most important sense a school can have. I work hard to get that sense, and that means involving everybody we can in just about everything."

This principal provided a climate conducive to problem solving and risk taking. He delivered on what he promised and ensured teachers, where possible, the resources they needed to do what they all agreed must be done. He also worked to make time available for planning and for the commitments that high TPA requires. He gave teachers decision-making authority and responsibility to work out issues they deemed necessary to their goals. He worked hard to promote positive attitudes toward change. One teacher characterized the principal as, "strict, stable, yet flexible. He is an understanding administrator who says and acts as if the teacher is the most important player on the team. He expects us to come up with new ideas and to push them. He says if we [teachers] don't do it, nobody will."

Another teacher reported that the leadership of the principal "has been liberating. It frees us to try new things and to be professionally responsible for them."

At Ruraldom, Goodlad (1984) would find a policy environment reflective of what he referred to as a paradigm shift regarding the traditional relations between teachers and administrators. He characterized the shift in these words:

> Leadership by authority is replaced by leadership by knowledge; following rules and regulations is replaced by providing more room for decision-making; mandated behavior is replaced by inquiring behavior; accountability is replaced by high expectations, responsibility, and a level of trust that includes freedom to make mistakes; and much more. (p.4)

Even with its unconventional governance and its astounding community support, Ruraldom was constrained by formal policy, law, and regulation. Like any public school, Ruraldom functioned in a system of statutory vertical organization, in which power and authority increased as one moved up the ladder from the classroom to the local school board, to the state legislature, and so on. However, due to tradition, trust in school professionals, and a record of success, great flexibility was exercised at Ruraldom compared with what was typical. This school and the professionals in it constituted living examples of what Goodlad had in mind.

The eschewing of formal or de jure authority in favor of custom, tradition, and de facto authority made the socialization of newcomers especially important. Veterans at Ruraldom knew this and acted on it; as they put it, "this place is so different from other schools that it is understood only by those of us in it." Accordingly, Ruraldom school professionals were scrupulous about the kind of colleague they recruited. In turn, induction and related socialization activities, for the professional as well as the student, were directed at conformity with the rules, regulations, and customs of the school.

That conformity was limiting; it denied the individualistic ethic typical of many high schools. Ruraldom constituted a village of common thought, beliefs, and values, and it aimed to continue to do so. Like the "successful" private high schools described by Powell and his colleagues (1986), Ruraldom was not shaped by conflicting values, competing beliefs, and radical individualism. It did not afford a wide range of choices among curricula, teaching styles, programs, values, or behaviors. It restricted or circumscribed diversity and choice and substituted for them single-mindedness of purpose, lean curricula, and common behavior in just about all matters, from teaching style to dress codes.

The high value placed on unity, conformity, and interdependency helped make Ruraldom a school whose essence was comprehensible, meaningful, enduringly purposeful, and directive for those who served it and were served by it. Students and teachers considered themselves fully integrated into a social order that embraced them. They shared a commitment to work together in a mutuality of interest. They shared not merely this or that interest, but a whole set of interests, wide enough and complete enough to include their personal as well as their professional lives. Theirs, then, was an integrated and harmonious world.

The configuration of traits linked to this community-like school was suggestive of what is known about organic community generally. The stability, benefits, and satisfaction of community depended on acceptance of authority, adherence to group-sanctioned belief, loyalty, and a willingness to subordinate individual identity to a communal identity.

Community generally demands habits of deference comfortable for individuals who have a high need for order and a low need for change. On the other hand, individuals in communities are protected and taken care of. They enjoy a rich sense of time and place, camaraderie, and belonging; these benefits may account for the high morale that was characteristic of RUHS.

The traits and dimensions that characterized Ruraldom Union High School constitute a delicately balanced but tightly knit fabric or system. If change was slow in this school, it was because of the many bases that had to be touched. But when change was effected, it was felt by all elements in the system.

The tightly knit character of this school made it complex. Noteworthy in this time of mandated reform, RUHS was resistant to change introduced from outside. The factors that appeared correlative to the efficacy of this school could be put at risk, vulnerable to damage or elimination by outside mandates for reform or change.

Reflect for a moment on some of the terms and phrases used to characterize the policy environment of Ruraldom and the people who make up that environment:

- trust, fraternal cooperation
- collaborative engagement
- shared responsibility
- collective psychological ownership
- interdependence
- shared beliefs and values
- common goals
- shared purpose
- consensual governance
- high teacher professional authority

- school as unique
- school as a countervailing force
- tightly knit
- moral authority

Cohen (1983) could have been describing Ruraldom when he wrote:

> The norms and values which characterize the school community, and which unite individual members of the organization into a . . . cohesive identity, pertain both to the academic function of the school, as well as to the nature of the day-to-day interactions and social relations among staff and students. . . . However, . . . community in schools is dependent upon more shared instrumental goals. It requires the creation of a *moral order*, which entails *respect for authority* . . . and the *consistent enforcement of norms* which *define* and *delimit* acceptable *behavior*. (p. 33; emphasis added)

Communities arise for different reasons, out of different conditions. By definition, however, a community is different from anything to which it could be compared. Members of Ruraldom had scant experience by which to make such comparison, but what they had seen justified their conviction that theirs was a special, unique, and superior place. Given the lives they shaped within the harsh circumstances they endured, even outsiders would see strong evidence to support their conviction.

Chapter 7

Townston Regional High School

I left the interstate, and the exit on the right guided me to a narrow, typical New England two-way highway. Low shoulders hugged by tall and stately elms, maples, and intermittent evergreens evoked the image of an inviting tunnel. Views beyond the roadway through breaks in the seeming forest offered rolling hills and cleared but no-longer tilled meadows dotted with clumps of trees. The forests at the edges were creeping to reclaim the rugged earth. It was bucolic; and it was short-lived. A bustling mix of new condominium and apartment developments, fast food strips, factory outlet malls, and traffic-clogged villages took over the landscape.

The area's major state thoroughfare transported me through an odd assortment of places and eras: a modern strip of highway, jammed with cars and trucks, framed by fast food restaurants, gas stations, car washes, and bars; then a Norman Rockwell village of long green lawns fronting white frame houses and white steepled churches; and streets bloated with bumper-to-bumper "rush hour" traffic; then a quiet, town business district suffering a loss of customers to the indoor shopping mall up the road.

The looming presence of the high school and its grounds dominated my field of vision as I approached the area of the school. It simply sprawled all over—flat, long, and spidery. The physical plant, comprised of several one-story connected buildings constructed as add-ons to the original two-story brick building, gave the appearance of a never-ending maze.

Carved out of the side of a small hill and surrounded by lush oak, birch, and maple trees, the Townston Regional High School campus subsumed eight acres, most of which were taken up by a parking lot made necessary, I was to learn later, by the number of students driving cars to school. "I would guess that there is one car for every three students," a guidance counselor was to tell me.

The building and the grounds would be the envy of many of the state college systems throughout New England; and a long, rectangular, windowless gym that would be coveted by many major universities was the largest single entity. The most interesting structure had a domed center roof, suggestive of the planetarium within (suggestive, that is, if one expected a planetarium within a public or, indeed, any high school).

Anchoring the southwestern corner of this lumbering complex were two all-glass greenhouses, "one for tropical and exotic plants, the other for domestic plants," a school board member was to explain proudly. "I'm not sure what the difference between a domestic and an exotic is, but we have a greenhouse for each." In terms of facilities alone, TRHS was truly an impressive place. Also impressive was the plethora of Saabs, BMWs, and Mercedeses in the student section of the parking lot. Clearly, there was no economic recession here.

CASE #2: TOWNSTON REGIONAL HIGH SCHOOL

Fact File

Total number of students: **1 5 0 0**   Grades: **9 - 1 2**

Ethnic composition: **96% white, 1% black, 1.5% Asian, 1.5% Hispanic**

Percentage from low income families: **1 . 6 %**

Number of staff:

	Full-Time	Part-Time	Other
Administrators	1 Prin.	2 Asst Prin.	
Teachers	8 1	4	
Teacher Aides	4	0	
Counselors	5	1	
Library/Media Staff	3	0	
Social Workers	0	1	
Security Officers	0	0	
Food Service Staff	0	1 0	
Clerical Staff	6	3	
Subject Area Specialists	8FT	4PT	

Percentage of professional staff with graduate degrees: **7 1 %**

Average length of service of professional staff: **9 years**

Organizational structure: **Departmental**

Selected outcomes of prior's years graduates:
   enrolled in four-year college or university: **7 2 %**
   enrolled in two-year college: **9 %**
   enrolled in vocational training: **6 %**
   employed full-time: **1 2 %**
   employed part-time: **0 %**
   enlisted in the military: **1 %**

Extracurricular participation rate: **8 7 %**

Drop-out rate: **2 %**

Average daily attendance rate: **9 4 . 5 %**

Average daily teacher attendance: **9 8 %**

Fifteen hundred students attended Townston Regional High School, described by its school officials in various public relations documents as a "comprehensive high school," and by its principal as the "best public prep school in the East." Comprehensive indeed. The school's curriculum was as expansive as the physical facilities. It was the residue of different reform eras and their imperatives, and academic trends generally since the school opened in 1953. Students could study several languages in depth. They could enroll in advanced courses and seminars in history, math, the sciences—offerings not available at the typical high school, nor in some colleges. Those so inclined could take courses in such high school exotica as astronomy, botany, psychology, sociology, and film; these courses promised content and experiences as engaging as those in any college catalogue. (I was reminded in this regard of the Ruraldom parent who cited the lack of a calculus course and advanced foreign language courses as the only weaknesses of the RUHS that he could call to mind.)

The majority of Townston's students were from two adjacent towns approximately 30 miles north and west of a major northeastern city. A few students, "between 40 and 50 a year for the past few years," according to the superintendent, were "tuitioned-in" from other towns. Their parents paid over $3,000 annually (in the mid 1980s) so that their children could attend this well-regarded high school. "There are some private schools in this part of the country that are less expensive," said a father of one of the "tuitioned" students, "but not too many, and few, if any, can match what this school can offer."

Through most of the 1950s, Townston had only about 3,500 residents. Its broad valleys and low hills, like most of postagricultural New England, were being reclaimed by forests. The residents of towns in the area had lived comfortably in and around several loosely connected villages. This began to change radically in the late 1950s. The populations of Townston and Greenbelt (the other town served by TRHS) doubled between 1950 and 1960, then doubled again during the next 10 years as the towns absorbed the white collar professionals brought into the area by high tech industries that sprouted along a nearby highway.

By 1970 the majority of people living in the towns served by TRHS likely came from someplace else and were just as likely not to stay. There was little "old money" in the communities TRHS served; what genuine wealth existed was concentrated in a small number of senior citizens.

Townston and Greenbelt remained self-contained residential communities with a combined population of about 25,000.

The burgeoning computer industries and an insurance company headquarters had brought in so many professionals and service industries that the area became the northeast's equivalent of Silicon Valley. "Escapees from the crime and grime of . . . [the city to the south] has added to the area's growth in population and its changing character," reported a school board member.

Schools reflect the communities and populations they serve, a reality that is often invoked as sufficient to account for each school's unique character. But "reflect" has different meanings. TRHS reflected its towns and their populations by mirroring them, whereas reflection for other schools might mean transcending or negating the towns they served. Townston Regional High School sought to ensure that its students adopted and maintained the values, ideals, and ambitions of their parents. As one parent put it: "Ambition is the byword in our towns. It is also the byword at the school."

This "mirroring" relationship was revealed in the initial impression TRHS made on me, principally through its ambience. Students at TRHS moved through its corridors in a friendly fashion. They laughed, touched, grabbed, pushed, and shoved. And they greeted me and other visitors amicably. But there was a studied aspect to their welcomes, a sense that they were doing what was expected. They were self-consciously polite. They moved through the hallways with purpose, doing the business of schooling. There was not even an appearance of loitering. There was no relaxed, "How you doing?", "May I show you around?", "Take you to someplace?" Indeed, if they lingered too long and were late for a class, a penalty was imposed, with no excuses accepted.

The hustle and bustle of the towns with their frenetic thoroughfares were reflected here. The ambience was certainly friendly, but the climate of TRHS did not convey the warmth and community I experienced at some schools.

TRHS demonstrated order and a cooperative atmosphere throughout the school. The buildings and grounds were in excellent condition, clean and well-maintained. A pride in keeping the building and grounds attractive was evidenced by custodians and students. Custodians reported that their charge, "to keep the place looking sharp," was "important to keeping up the standards and high quality of this school." The "people in this area expect the school to look good. If it didn't, the principal would hear from them, and we would hear from the principal."

TRHS did not suffer from a shortage of custodial staff and contractual services for keeping the building and grounds in excellent condition. It had sufficient help through full-time custodial staff and contractual services with local providers to maintain its building and grounds in superb condition.

"We have several booster clubs associated with athletics and with other activities," explained the principal. "They raise money for special equipment, programs, and landscaping that we wouldn't be able to do otherwise."

Students pointed out that most of the appealing art work throughout the halls of the building was the work of students. Some was on loan from people in the community; some was owned by the school, given by community benefactors. "Some of these [paintings and sculptures] are worth quite a few dollars," said a guidance counselor. "We talk about the dollar value now and then. With expensive stuff you've got to be careful."

Faculty pride in the school and in themselves was evident. It was expressed in ways which, although acknowledging the important place of teachers in decision making, emphasized the centrality of teaching roles over policy-making roles. A teacher on a "school climate" task force put it this way: "Creating a climate conducive to learning has been a primary goal of this school. Good climate requires pride. To be able to take pride in your place of work requires that your work be important and respected. And it is respected here; we insist on it. Above all it is our work as teachers, as classroom instructors, that is the most important thing about us and this school."

The business-like ambience related to and was reflected in other aspects of the school. For example, the goal and mission statements and other elements that comprised Townston's policy environment (see Table 7.1) depicted values of individualism and hard work.

"All schools expect hard work more or less," observed a chemistry teacher, "and all schools preach about values regarding the work ethic. But the influence of these expectations depends upon how they fit the school. We make sure that what we say and do is connected, so that everything is strengthened."

An individualistic ethic dominated the policy elements of TRHS. The solitary ego who could enjoy independence through hard work and self reliance was the favored personality type. For example, student privileges did not come with mere movement through the system as they do at many public schools. They did not simply accrue to the more senior students as is the case in most public high schools. Privileges had to be earned, and students who earned points on the way to privileges were granted some relief from the constraints of rules and regulations. "Just like life," explained one junior. "Privileges must be earned to enjoy benefits."

Table 7.1. The Policy Environment of Townston Regional High School.

<u>MISSION</u>:	*To prepare students for a lifetime of learning by offering rigorous, high quality academic studies combined with academic, personal, and career counseling.*
<u>AMBIENCE</u>:	*A friendly, sophisticated, and fast-paced atmosphere that conveys a palpable sense of pride, efficiency, and confidence.*
<u>ETHOS</u>:	*An individualistic logic favoring the solitary, independent ego; a competitive ethic prevails, fostering a strongly felt spirit of friendly competition and achievement.*
<u>GOVERNANCE</u>:	*A hierarchical, mechanistic, and formal pattern; numerous committees exist, and representation from all professional and nonprofessionals in the school is mandated.*
<u>ORGANIZATIONAL CONTROL</u>:	*Bureaucratic, formal, and hierarchical with de jure authority ruling.*
<u>LEADERSHIP</u>:	*Confined to position in the echelon. It is exercised primarily <u>de jure</u>; principal as the statutory and customary leader is primary in answering to and in directing others.*
<u>TEACHER PROFESSIONAL AUTHORITY</u>	*Covers many program and policy areas and is exercised through mandated representation on committees; TPA is valued, given the professional respect it reflects and earns. But policymaking role is made secondary to teaching responsibilities.*
<u>SOCIALIZATION</u>:	*Left to positions in echelon; <u>de facto</u> and <u>de jure</u> support for the solitary ego; vital, competitive ethic encourages the exercise of individual philosophy, style, and personality.*
<u>MORAL AUTHORITY</u>:	*Confidence in academic quality reinforced by perception that school delivers on its promises; history of documented success makes the school credible among all its publics.*

Excellent grades and display of good work or behavior brought privileges such as early dismissal, or free passes to selected school or town events. Merely being a senior, even though that reflected achievement and attainment, did not bring these kinds of privileges. "We think our students must learn that it takes a lot of work and truly distinctive performance, whatever it's in, to get attention and win," explained a teacher of history.

The ambience and ethos of TRHS derived from the culture and values of the towns it served. Interpersonal relations between teachers and students, among students, and between teachers and administrators were cordial and business-like. They did not signal strong personal ties that derived from being members of a community. I heard no talk of "family" or "community" at this school.

The language of self-study documents, the Student Handbook, and teachers' and students' talk did not reflect the valuing of community and fraternity. Relationships here were transactional, not interactional. Energy and dedication were therefore focused on teaching and on courses that aimed at higher-order thinking skills or special abilities. All this, like the ambience itself, derived from the values of the towns served by TRHS.

The parents of Townston's students had grown accustomed to moving on to get ahead, and to staying ahead. The idea of fast, limitless improvement leading to ever-increasing success was a powerful motivating belief among these parents. Important to that idea was the notion of moving up and out.

Many were like John Ambrose, who struggled to support himself on his way to becoming the first college graduate in his family. Ambrose and his wife, an English teacher at TRHS, came to the area within the prior three to six years. They were like other recent arrivals in the area. Men were primarily professionals in high tech and insurance businesses, and women tended to work at home, or in the service professions as librarians, social workers, nurses, or teachers at TRHS and other schools in the system.

John Ambrose's electrical engineering degree brought him to a major computer firm. His company invested in him in various ways, including paying his tuition and related expenses so that he might earn an MBA at a near-by university. Ambrose spoke for many parents of TRHS students when he explained what he wanted from schooling for his children.

Education and the credentials it got me did everything for me. . . . I worked hard. My folks gave me all the moral and material support they could. But they had no idea of what college was all about. I had to do it myself. I'm not bragging;

I'm just saying that hard work, finding out for yourself,
learning to depend upon yourself will get you what you want.
I want my kids' schools to teach them these things. I think
our school is doing that. That's why I support it so much,
why I'm a booster. . . .

The values reflected in Ambrose's statement were reinforced by the responses of other parents and by a characteristic
many of the parents shared: mobility—upward, in terms of social
status, and moving on, in terms of going where the company wanted and needed them. The Ambroses had moved several times before,
and they were likely to move again.

Another set of parents enjoyed telling me how years ago
they had been in the twin cities, where they spent eight years. In
the years since, they and their children had "been two years in
Poughkeepsie, two years in Cincinnati, one year in Louisville, and
two years in [Townston]. We are probably going to have to move
next year."

"Moving is so much a part of the lives of our children that
we really need to rely upon the schools not only to help them
adjust to each move but to make sure they are getting the best
academics. They need the best," reported a mother of twins.

Perhaps the fact that there did not seem to be a strong need
for community in the school was a function of the premium placed
on independence and mobility. A teacher of English claimed as
much when he observed: "There's not much to be gained from cul-
tivating community when many students and some teachers will
move before long. Why build esprit when you aren't going to be
around? In fact, if your school is truly like a community, what's
it like for the newcomer? Harder to get in, isn't it?"

A parent observed: "What we all need is to get the most out
of this place while we can, and that is what the school tries to do
for us." The school was the place in which parents invested in the
shaping of their children's future. And the investment was associated with an individualistic, competitive ethic.

As might be expected, the socialization of newcomers,
teachers, and students alike favored individualism. There was little effort aimed at making Townston's professionals and students
members of a village of common thought. "It seems to me,"
observed a department chair, "that a push for building a common
purpose, for creating some kind of community, can be infantiliz-
ing and stifling, especially with a transient population like ours.
It wouldn't work here."

A language teacher put it this way: "We want to benefit

from each other's strengths. So we look for faculty who can complement other faculty. We try to get the most from individual special interests and talents."

TRHS was nevertheless committed to formal socialization activities for its newcomers. Teachers served as mentors to new teachers, and several orientation and in-service training sessions were held during the school year to ensure that teachers were well inducted into TRHS. This approach seemed to fit the needs and desires of administrators and teachers at Townston. "It gives everybody what they expect and want," reported an assistant to the principal. Interviews and informal talks with teachers confirmed this perspective.

The lack of emphasis on community and the business-like approach to the socialization of teachers were congruent with other aspects of TRHS, including the place of parents in school policy and decision making. One of the first things that parents reported to me was that they had more than enough access to the principal and the staff, to "have ourselves heard, if we feel the need," as one parent put it. A school board member pointed out that numerous opportunities existed for parent and community involvement in the school. These included parent advisory groups, parent volunteer groups, use of the school building by the community through adult education courses [over 600 attended per semester], recreational activities, parent-teacher conferences, a district-wide newsletter, several TRHS publications, frequent open houses, and good access to the school board. "They know what we want and our kids need," he said, "and they provide it."

In some ways, TRHS was evocative of a kind of university or college wherein community inclination was disdained as antithetical to an ethic of independence and where young people were expected to fend for themselves. A writer for a publication in the region of Townston noted: "Our High School has replaced the church in terms of where parents place their greatest faith . . . [relative to influencing their children's futures]."

Parents believed strongly that TRHS was a good school because, as one father put it, "it has a good blend of academic and other activities. This school brings out the best in my children and, from what I can tell, in others as well. I certainly know that they are challenged to do the work that is necessary to get them into the college they want."

Parents and other townspeople expressed the belief that a sound basic and general education, solid grounding in academics, and opportunities for all students to develop their capacities were crucial to a good learning environment. "Everyone in the area knows this is a demanding school," reported the father of a track star. "It gives our kids a good solid grounding in academics and offers chances to develop other talents, too."

Among other distinguishing features, Townston was characterized by attention to data. School administrators used data for planning, such as targeting goals and tracking progress, local fundraising efforts through booster clubs, proposals to the state and sometimes to the federal government for grants, and motivating school groups to outdo previous performances. They also used data in ways that enhanced the school's reputation. For example, the school's application for the SSRP noted (and I later confirmed) that "there is no grade inflation at TRHS. Only 6.3%, 7.6%, and 5.2% of all grades given during the past three years were As. And during those same years, 13%, 11.6%, and 12.4% were Ds and Fs."

Townston's teachers were proud of their tough grading practices. They were also proud of the fact that 87% of TRHS students took SATs, contrasted with about 60% of the students in the state. TRHS students performed well above state and national averages.

A four-page document from the Townston school system titled *Evidence of Excellence* was distributed widely to prospective home buyers. It read like a prospectus from a top prep school as it announced that:

> Many high schools claim to have excellent programs. A few are able to offer concrete evidence of their excellence. [Townston] is one that can. We have chosen to compare our students to students throughout the nation, our regional area, and to students in other specific high schools which traditionally have been thought to have excellent programs. Although test scores are only one limited type of evidence, we believe this evidence shows that graduates of [Townston Regional High School] had a superior education.

The document reported that its most recent graduating class "ranked third statewide on the SATs," that on the recent California Achievement Tests, the "average 6th grader [in the Townston system] scored higher than 92% of students nationally in reading, language, and math," and that "parents of 44 students from surrounding towns paid over $3,000 to send their children to Townston schools."

The document also reported that Townston graduates' scores on various aspects of the SATs demonstrated much better performance on average than graduates of two high schools reputed to be among the very best in the country, and much better on average than graduates of 10 highly regarded suburban high schools in the state. This publication included comparisons of College Board test scores and percentages of students enrolled in Advanced Placement Programs. Among the schools compared with Townston were Evanston (IL) Township High School and Newton (MA) High School. Townston compared very favorably.

Evidence of Excellence was an impressive document, not only in terms of what it reported, but in terms of the manner of reporting. Pride came to mind first. Hubris was also evoked.

A mother told me that she valued the school because "it forces kids to extend themselves and to commit to excellence. I can drop my daughter off at 6:45 in the morning and know that someone will be here to give her the extra help and encouragement she is looking for."

Above all else, the parents emphasized the strong academics of this school. "The school provides a broad academic program for our kids," said one parent. "Over 90% are taking courses that will prepare them for college. It also offers an excellent business training program."

"In some ways," reported a father who was a graduate of a large midwestern state university, "this place has the feel and tone of the kind of small liberal arts college I imagined but never got the chance to attend."

The emphasis on academics that parents expected from TRHS was not solely a function of a grand and highly idealistic philosophy of education. The set of beliefs that drove Townston was pragmatic. Lofty slogans and high-minded ideals were not part of the oral reports about TRHS, nor were they written in various self-study and other documents.

"We do not try to be coy in terms of our philosophy; we don't trivialize it with empty slogans," reported a school board member. "[Townston] gives our children the opportunity to take subject matter that will get them in good colleges. That's what it promises, that's what it does. That's what most of us want."

Parents testified to their satisfaction with the school by pointing to ways they supported it. Some indicated the widespread parental involvement in various school volunteer groups, the activities of the various booster clubs, attendance at sports events, and school plays. "We show our support for this school by doing what we can. We gave over $160,000 last year to what we call the Townston Students Activities Fund. It helped support sports and arts programs that might not get as much support from the school budget. It allows the school to offer things it might otherwise not be able to and to offer those things it does in a better or more classy way."

Another parent added: "About $75,000 in local scholarship money will given out at graduation this year."

Townston school professionals, as well as the parents, were very proud of these achievements in community support for the school. Its administrators and parent advisory groups were adept at keeping that pride at a high level. They produced publications that documented the source of monies for and the nature of "[Townston] Local Scholarships." Those publications reported on previous years' dollar amounts and provided statistical analyses and graphic portrayals of these that captured interest and motivated people to make each year's outcome better than the last.

Getting its charges into a "good" college accounted for much of the energy and time spent by professionals at TRHS. TRHS published a *College Planning Handbook* for its students and their parents, "to help TRHS juniors and seniors plan for their future." The Counseling and Guidance Staff published a newsletter, *Communique*, which emphasized college-bound concerns. Topics such as "Applying to College," "College Planning Timetable," "Transition to College," and the like were addressed in these publications.

On over 120 school days of the 190-day school year, admissions officers from various colleges and universities were at Townston. "Advising students about college, helping them to arrange interviews with some of them, and getting them into the college or university of their choice is the major job of the guidance and counseling staff," reported the principal. One parent was quoted in a local publication as saying that the "SAT results show years of grooming and preparation. If you haven't got the PSATs nailed down in the 10th grade, give it up."

Several teachers told me (affirmed proudly by the guidance staff) that students were, as one put it, "excused from our classes all the time, but it gets really hectic during the recruitment seasons."

A parent who did not quite fit the norm said that he "found the whole orientation toward success very oppressive. I must admit, though, that most parents welcome it." He regretted that "our highest expectations fall upon the young shoulders of our kids. There is a relentless pressure to make it that is put upon these kids."

Competition was the most obvious way pressure to perform was translated into behavior. "Competition is favored around

here, given the results, the achievements," reported one suburban mother. This pride and the competitive character of the
school's ethos was reflected in the earlier cited publication,
Evidence of Excellence, in a section that compared Townston's
performance with that of several other schools, primarily those
with reputations for "excellence."

The only staff person who spoke critically of the school's
emphasis on college-bound academics was the lone industrial arts
teacher. Historically, TRHS had offered its own vocational education program. However, since the mid 1970s, students interested
in a vocational-technical education had to attend a regional "voc-
tech" center. Students interested in woodwork, auto mechanics, or
other courses associated with vocational education could take a
course or two at TRHS, but this option, too, was in the process of
being eliminated during the early 1980s. "I am on my way out
because there are no students. There are no students because there
are no classes for them. There are no classes because they have
been slowly but surely cut out of the schedules over the past
years. I don't think it's right. The other shop teachers [there
were four] have left over the last five or six years. When I'm
gone there will be nobody. If a kid wants to take a course, he can't.
He has to be a voc-tech major and go somewhere else for part of
the day. This is hard to do. It's not right."

It may not have been right, but no objections other than
this teacher's were voiced to me.

Table 7.1 depicts the overall policy environment of
Townston Regional High School. It indicates that Townston was
characterized by an organizational structure that was bureaucratic, hierarchical, and efficient. The logic of other policy elements suggested—indeed, made predictable—such a structure.
Ambience, ethos, mission, TPA, and other elements suggested,
reflected, and supported this dominant theme.

Townston's policy environment gave all the appearance of an
efficient operation governed by rationalistic, formal, and highly specific policy. The authority for governance, indeed for most things at
TRHS, arose formally. Authority and responsibility were exercised
through positions given those qualities by statute. Nearly everything
relating to life in this school was covered by policy. Written rules
and regulations addressed just about all realms of behavior, from
receiving and hosting visitors to storing chalk. The mobility of people
required the stability and endurance of the written word.

The consequence of all this was a clear division of labor
enshrined in formal policy and honored in practice. The principal

and his administrative assistants functioned in a manner traditionally associated with the principalship; they were granted a great deal of power by virtue of their position. The principal was not a first among equals; he was first. His overall aim, reported in language befitting his view of his role, was "to make this high school a model for others. Maybe not for all schools, not for those that are in the ghettos, but for just about all others. I am competitive and assertive. I want to keep this school on top, after we have worked so hard to get there."

Teachers, students, and parents acknowledged the principal's power and his place in guiding the school to its present status. A long-time department chair reported that he "came here about 15 years ago, just about the time this area was really beginning to change. He took charge right from the beginning, bringing in parents and university consultants. This place has always been a decent school. But we never had so much of an academic bent and so many of our graduates going on. It was more laid back in the old days. Dr. Kendra (not his real name) made it much more organized. There is no doubt in my mind that he had a sense of what this area was going to be like and he responded by working to make the school fit that situation."

The principal himself confirmed what others reported about him and his role in making TRHS what it had become. "Many of my efforts have been aimed at getting this place to the point where all kids get a kind of high school equivalent of a liberal arts program. And I have used the power of the principalship to do that. I am in a position of authority and I use it."

Given this context, it is surprising that teacher professional authority was as extensive, as important to teachers, and as consequential as it was. Teachers had an influential but not necessarily decisive voice over curricular, instructional, and discipline policy. Also, teachers were represented on the various study groups and task forces that helped set school directions and goals. The teacher evaluation process was fashioned jointly by faculty and administration. "We have a decisive voice in most building policy," reported a teacher of math. "I think we, teachers, are much more important in policy than we were eight, ten years ago."

TPA was exercised here at schoolwide, departmental, and program levels through a representative governance arrangement. All standing committees, ad hoc committees, and task forces included department and program representatives by statute. These representatives were typically "elected" by having volunteered. Those selected to schoolwide groups were expected to represent themselves. They were not obligated to represent a department's or program's agenda. They were, however, expected to report to the groups from which they were elected and to explain and sometimes defend their positions on issues of interest. Even at the departmental or program level, business was done through formal committees.

The school's main legislative body was the faculty as a whole. Faculty members met regularly with the administration to receive, discuss, and take action on recommendations that came from various committees and task forces. "The real influence of teachers is on the committees," reported a department chair. "The large legislative body is a place to listen to recommendations and receive information."

As with so many aspects of TRHS, TPA was protected by formal policy, which declared that "no decisions are made on curriculum, instruction, or discipline policy without the direct involvement and vote of faculty." "We may not always live up to that policy," claimed a biology teacher. "We may not always take it seriously, but for the most part it is practiced."

Even though TPA existed through formal policy, was comparatively extensive, and acknowledged as important, teachers were not as protective of it as might be expected. One teacher explained her position this way: "Administrators are paid to deal with most of this business, anyway. Why should we get bogged down in it? Let's use our influence to get the right conditions for teaching, not to be burdened with administrivia. It's the administration that should spend its time on that, and we are supposed to instruct kids."

Other teachers at TRHS expressed the view that the only efficient way to make decisions was to leave responsibility with administrators and representatives who were interested in or knowledgeable about particular committees. "We are not interested in becoming administrators," a history teacher said. "We should not want to spend our time other than teaching and thinking about teaching. You can't be a teacher and a policymaker or administrator and do well at both."

A department chairperson wanted me to know that he "and just about everybody knows that teachers work very hard, too hard. But when we talk in the lounge, we all agree that is a healthy kind of hard work. It pays off for our students and we have fewer tensions around here than you might expect."

Teachers insisted, however, that formal protection of TPA was important to them, even if they did not always take full advantage nor demand more of it. "It is crucial for us as professionals to have our voice and our role in policy development stated formally;

if it weren't, the principal would ignore us. He can't, now."

"That's probably true," conceded the principal when asked about this comment. "I've been here for 15 years, and I think I know this place pretty well . . . what it needs, what makes it run well, what teachers need and want, and so on. And if left to my own devices, I probably wouldn't spend much time checking things out with teachers—on what you call professional authority matters."

Teacher autonomy, associated with the discretionary authority teachers enjoy in their classrooms, was highly valued and protected at TRHS. Appreciation of this kind of autonomy reinforced the lack of emphasis on community and collective professional authority. Thus at TRHS, governance was less self-government by a collegium and more governance by committee.

Teachers spent a great deal of their time together talking about teaching and about their courses. They also spent time discussing professional development matters. Continuing education and remaining current on developments in their fields were more important than governance or "internal politics."

Teacher supervision maintained individual autonomy and satisfaction with the individualistic status quo. Teacher evaluations were formal and conducted within the context framed by the negotiated contract. The evaluation of all professionals rested on valuing individualism and diversity. It was the kind of diversity that was supportive of a competitive ethic.

This kind of diversity woven with teacher autonomy and with a formalistic policy environment described Townston Regional High School and the professionals in it. Teacher loyalties were directed to their disciplines, to teaching obligations, and to student academic needs. Concern for people was the responsibility of individuals rather than the system. "When a teacher is laid-up we don't send flowers funded by a school-wide pool, as in a lot of places," said the principal. "We don't express our sympathy through a card that a secretary buys and we all sign. Individuals can choose to respond or not. I will bring the situation to everyone's attention over the intercom if it's appropriate, but response is up to individuals."

The combination of a clear division of labor, representative governance, an individualistic ethic, and transience (evidenced to some extent in the faculty, but primarily among the students) produced an ambience that suggested a place of business. At Townston Regional High School, as in the region from which it sprang, business was defined narrowly by position and role. It followed that policy, program development, and implementation were initiated and carried out with teacher input in its formally designated place.

School professionals expressed their responsibilities to students in language that conveyed their sense of professional, academic, or vocational obligation, as opposed to personal interest. "Parents and other family members can and should do the loving and caring for their children. Our job is to educate them for college and life," commented a teacher of French.

Townston professionals were not coldly uninterested in their students. A guidance counselor commented, noting that "individual teachers certainly are interested in serving and supporting students in more personal ways, but it's up to the individual. It is not policy. Some institutions like the family, church, and social services agencies have to take care of that side of the student's life. Our job is to make sure that our students receive the best academic and career preparation our school can offer."

The principal agreed. "The primary need of all our students is for strong academics. About 90% of our students plan on college. Both students and parents want a program that focuses on academics."

Several teachers reported that the principal was always working to keep the academic mission of TRHS in the thoughts of teachers, students, and parents. "He sometimes hands out one-page statements that speak to this overall goal," reported a teacher of biology. "He talks about it whenever questions about who we are come up."

The guidance counselor reported that the ways the school's mission is interpreted "are based on measures such as student surveys, parent comments, discussions with teachers, counselors, and students, and analyses of trends—what's going on in the country, statewide, and the like. Our data collection is supplemented by surveys of former students done every five years."

In this context, and especially in light of the clientele served, it should come as no surprise that the overall purpose of Townston Regional High School was articulated this way:

> to prepare students for lifelong learning by offering high quality academic studies combined with academic, personal and career counseling.

This purpose, expressed in a variety of ways, appeared in school documents, including self-studies, statements of instructional goals, and a detailed curriculum guide used by students and their parents to ensure compliance with programs of study. These "instructional goals of the school" were expressed this way:

to provide an atmosphere in which learning is encouraged, and to help students recognize that education is a process of which their present experience is only a small part

to meet the common educational needs of the students and, to the extent . . . possible and desirable, to meet their individual needs, aptitudes, and interests

to make students aware . . . they are able to and must responsibly direct their own social and psychological evolution

to recognize every student as an individual and to encourage the student to think of him/herself as a contributing member of a changing society and to appreciate the life styles of others

to aid students in the recognition of their moral rights and responsibilities, and the need to adhere to them

to guide students in the development of habits and attitudes which will result in sound moral and psychological health, appreciation of what is appropriate in the arts and in the art of living, knowledge and skills that will make them intelligent and responsible citizens of the community and the world . . . , skills and abilities that will serve them as consumers and producers in our economic system

to encourage a gradual development of each student's ability to approach, analyze, and solve tomorrow's problems and to express themselves in a variety of ways, . . . to separate facts from fiction, assume self responsibility, recognize their abilities and limitations.

In response to questions about these goals, the principal reported that, although quite general on their face, "they have been translated into instructional objectives in the written curriculum guides of each department. These objectives are clear, measurable, and are at the heart of an accountability system that strives for valid and reliable evaluations. Curriculum guides are available to students and parents and written summaries are distributed at the Back to School Nights which have overflow turnouts."

The goals were originally developed in 1980 through a process that involved a group of parents, students, teachers, and administrators, and were approved by the school board. An annual review of the goals was conducted by teachers and administrators to determine if they warranted revision.

The individualistic ethic at TRHS, supported by an overall mission expressed in academic and career terms, was reinforced by practices that were clearly in the direction of individual achievement and attainment. A seemingly incidental but contextually important feature of Townston was revealed in the fact that individual sports at TRHS were overenrolled. This was no accident. Individual sports and interscholastic academic competitions were heavily favored. Individual winners were celebrated and honored, consistent with the individualistic ethic of the school and the community.

The statement from the principal in the *Student Handbook* reflected the school's pride in what it expected of students:

> If you have talked with employers in business and industry, admissions personnel in colleges and universities, I am sure you are aware of the fact that you are attending an outstanding secondary school. . . . [Townston], thanks to outstanding support from the community, has remarkable educational facilities, a comprehensive academic curriculum, diverse extracurricular programs, and an excellent teaching and extracurricular staff. Over the years, . . . [Townston] graduates have been highly successful throughout the nation. The effort, attitude, motivation, and success of the [Townston] graduate has made all of us associated with [Townston] very aware of the fact that we have much more than community support, superb facilities, fine programs, and an excellent staff—we have outstanding young people attending [Townston]. If we are to continue this legacy of pride and tradition, we must all realize that learning is a contractual endeavor necessitating maximum effort from all parties.

Townston's performance lived up to its promise. The college bound rate suggested that this public high school was more successful at preparatory school goals than most public schools and even private schools. Indeed, a list of the prestigious colleges and universities attended by a high percentage of Townston's graduates was as impressive as that of many status-conscious private preparatory schools—some of the most prestigious of which are not far from this public regional high school.

It is this efficacy that gave Townston Regional High School its moral authority. It derived such authority from the congruence between its goals, the expectations of its publics, and the realization of its goals. During the 5-year period of this study, over 80% of Townston graduates went on to higher education, the majority of them to 4-year institutions.

Success at Townston got students into the "good" colleges or universities they were promised. Thus, the school's capacity to have its values and beliefs accepted by students and parents was high. The moral authority of Townston, although different in character and function from that of Ruraldom, was just as potent.

Chapter 8

Cityville High School

The traffic picked up quite rapidly as I approached Cityville, a fishing, boat-building, and small manufacturing city with a metropolitan area population that totaled close to 300,000.

I sensed the sea long before I could see it while driving on the highway that led into this peninsula city. It was reflected in the dull gray sky, and I felt the chill of the Atlantic in the air that drifted into the open window of my car.

I turned off the highway at the street exit the principal had directed me to and, using a church steeple visible in the skyline, guided myself to the school.

It looked as if the school and its grounds occupied a couple of acres or so, just off a major downtown street. The school was in a neighborhood that had been in decline for some time. A few private dilapidated frame houses were on the four streets that framed the school. A grocery store with a delicatessen, a three-story parking garage, several warehouse-like buildings, and off-street parking lots comprised most of the immediate surrounding area. Three blocks beyond the school brought one into either residential areas or prime downtown business areas.

Cityville was not in a bucolic setting. Its surroundings were "city-ugly," as one Cityville High School junior was to describe it to me. However, the exterior of the building was magnificent.

The main edifice, constructed of pressed brick with granite and freestone trimming, was connected to three wings made of similar materials, resulting in an E-shaped structure. The protrusion in the middle of this imaginary capital E was the main entrance to the building. All wings were four-story structures, each with quotations, mostly from Shakespeare, carved into granite that framed seven major ground floor entrances. Gargoyles were embedded in concrete about halfway up and at the four major corners of each structure. They appeared to rest atop the granite trim. The quotations, arched over the major entrances, were marked further by red brick laid vertically over rounded pieces of red, black, and gray dotted granite.

This building looked like an academic institution, worthy of what citizens who designed and paid for it probably expected of a high school, known in those early days as the "people's college."

CASE #3: CITYVILLE HIGH SCHOOL

Fact File

Total number of students: **1 , 2 1 8**   Grades: **9 - 1 2**

Ethnic composition: **87% white, 3.0% black, 3.6% Asian, 3.5% Hispanic, 2.9 native American**

Percentage from low income families: **4 5 %**

Number of staff:

	Full-Time	Part-Time	Other
Administrators	1 Prin.	2 Asst Prin.	
Teachers .	7 5	6	
Teacher Aides	3	0	
Counselors	4		
Subject Area Specialists (e.g., Reading Spec)	2	6	
Library/Media Staff	1	0	
Social Workers	1	3	
Security Officers	0		
Food Service Staff	1	8	
Clerical Staff	6	0	

Percentage of professional staff with graduate degrees: **4 7 %**

Average length of service of professional staff: **1 1 years**

Organizational structure: **Program area clusters**

Selected outcomes for prior year's graduates:
enrolled in four-year college or university: **4 0 %**
enrolled in two-year college: **2 %**
enrolled in vocational training: **6 %**
employed full-time: **4 5 %**
employed part-time: **5 %**
enlisted in the military: **2 %**

Extracurricular participation rate: **7 4 %**

Dropout rate: **2 %**

Average daily student attendance: **9 0 . 6 %**

Average daily teacher attendance: **9 6 %**

Cityville High School was imposing because it was majestic. The main building evoked an image of what high schools were supposed to look like, if thinking was inspired by the architecture of American city high schools designed in the 19th and early 20th centuries.

"One of the oldest school buildings in the country," reported the principal proudly in response to my comments about it. "After Boston Latin, [Cityville] is probably the oldest public high school in the country. Some have tried to argue that we are the oldest. We can trace our origins back to 1821 when the city school committee organized a Latin School for boys who had graduated from grammar school."

The most impressive middle portion of the school building was constructed in 1863. The rest of the building was referred to as "the wings," which were constructed in 1918 and 1919.

"There is a great deal of history to this school, and we use it to impress students and visitors alike," a program head reported. "The school board has published an attractive pamphlet, A History of Cityville High School, distributed as a gift to visitors and required reading for all incoming freshmen," he continued.

The interior of the building was similarly impressive. There were long, spacious, energy-inefficient halls. Pine wood that was stained dark mahogany and 14-foot arched ceilings and granite walls and floors constituted the hallways. Classroom ceilings were also high in the old building, except for some laboratories and the main library where the ceilings had been lowered.

The central corridor, opening to the offices of the principal and assistant principals, was lined with portraits and large photographs of notable graduates. The stern faces of 19th- and early 20th-century men, along with the smiling faces of more modern notables (also all men), confronted those who passed through these halls. There were a world class explorer, a famous movie director, a professional athlete, a writer of popular fiction, and graduates who were killed in various wars from the Spanish-American to Vietnam. It was an impressive array. I wondered if the students were as inured to them as they appeared to be during their coming and going between classes.

An English teacher said, "if you ask students about this gallery, as we call it, you will probably discover that they know about it. Incoming freshmen classes are given an orientation to [Cityville]. It includes a formal guided tour through this hall, talks about the gallery that are given by students and teachers, and a distribution of our history book. Juniors are selected by the faculty to make presentations on grades, leadership, that sort of thing. It is considered an honor."

The idea behind this aspect of the orientation was to instill a sense of pride among students about the tradition of Cityville. "Some respond and are inspired as we would hope. But these are kids. Even those most moved by all this soon forget it," reported the principal in a conversation with me. "Maybe most kids can take it or leave it, but not adults and graduates who come back to reunions. They come in here and walk the halls. We get a lot out of this building and our history. Tradition is important here. History is important. We teach these things, and the building helps."

Paintings by current and former students hung in the gallery of portraits and photographs, along with paintings that were given to the school as gifts. "Most visitors are impressed," claimed an assistant principal. "Recent appraisals of the paintings pleased the school board immensely. There is a lot of money on these walls," he boasted. "There are not too many public high schools that have been around as long as ours. Also, most schools are not interested in their history. We take pride in it and try to pass it on to others."

Cityville was noisy and rambunctious when students and teachers moved through the halls before and after classes. I sensed informality and diversity here. Cityville's raucous spirit contrasted with the interior formality of the building.

Students and teachers were welcoming, but no special attention nor interest were evident. My earlier site visitor role had not evoked any special attention, and my "researcher-in-residence" status similarly produced neither anxiety, concern, nor particular interest. "You should know," reported the principal in an early conversation during my extended visit, "that our being in the Education Department's competition for recognition was the superintendent's idea. We did all the paperwork at his insistence. Most here couldn't care less. It's not that we didn't think we were good and deserving, but we have a jaded view of these things. We just have so much to do. Keeping ourselves on top of our day-to-day business is enough. Filling out forms for special awards that may help the system overall is nice, and we tried to be cooperative, but it wasn't a priority."

CHS was one of two public senior high schools in the city of Cityville, which was on a peninsula. Seagulls perched atop downtown skyscrapers, and there was a pervasive sense of the sea. The city was the financial, cultural, and retail center for the state and for other parts of New England. Tourism had also become a major industry during the last 15 years, due to the restoration of many parts of the city's historical district. Fifty-seven percent of Cityville's population were in white collar occupations; 29% were in blue collar occupations; and 13% were in service occupations.

Both city high schools were open enrollment schools. No particular feeder schools were designated for either. Parents and students were free to choose one school or the other on a first come, first served basis. "We and they have about the same enrollment," reported an assistant principal. "We could certainly take several more students, but we began the school year above our 1,200 or so comfortable enrollment. We have never had a problem with the enrollment choice approach."

Both schools were feeling the effects of the decline in high school-age population experienced across the country in the early 1980s. During the 1960s and throughout most of the 1970s, Cityville and the other high school had student populations of about 500 more than their enrollments during the early and mid 1980s.

Both schools were recognized in the area, within the State, and at the national level as good schools. Both were winners in the Secondary School Recognition Program. But the similarities appeared to end there. Although it was in the city, the other school was remarkably suburban in character and "not of the city" (hence "Outtown High School") as one proud CHS parent exclaimed. It was constructed in the 1950s and resembled most of the schools built during those years—one story, sprawling, red brick—"cheap, motel look-alike," as one Cityville parent described it. "Its student body is like the building," exclaimed another, "bland!" It was true that the population of Outtown High School was remarkably homogeneous in this city of ethnic, racial, and economic diversity.

The city of Cityville had long been an important fishing and boat-building center on the east coast, and over the years it had attracted large numbers of white ethnic groups, as well as Hispanic and Asian groups. The presence of a relatively large African-American population in the city and at CHS was explained by history as well. Some wealthy fishing and boat-building businessmen had extravagant homes during the 18th through the mid-20th centuries. Their money, homes, and lifestyles generated a demand for domestic help, and the city as a whole needed unskilled laborers. African Americans emigrated from the south through Boston and Hartford to this coastal city to fill those jobs.

My interview inquiries combined with documentation provided by the Cityville School System indicated that parents and students chose Cityville over its crosstown rival because of its cultural and social class diversity, the tolerance it had for the expression of individualism, the reputation of its performing and fine arts programs, the range and diversity of its curricular offerings, and the athletic success of the school. "Cityville is known throughout the Northeast. It produces great basketball players and super track athletes. Sports are wonderful to come here and watch," beamed the proud parent of one of the school's superstars. "It has helped a lot of kids get to college who wouldn't have been able to without scholarships."

Others selected Cityville for convenience. They lived within walking distance or a short ride away by car or bus. Some chose the school because of its setting and access to the city and its resources. "Because of the school's location in the heart of the city, our students have access to the city's best resources, from the modern public library and art museums to commercial and cultural resources," reported the superintendent.

The phrase "the city is our campus" appeared over the school's logo on all CHS publications. In turn, the school served as the center of many community activities that ranged from meetings for civic groups and city-sponsored athletic leagues to community player groups that needed the school's auditorium.

The halls were empty and quiet during classes, but they exploded with noise and movement between classes. Some students moved rapidly, some even ran; shouts of "cut it out" were heard. Others meandered. Still others pushed and shoved, started and stopped. Some students held hands, others hugged and kissed.

The cacophony left me with the positive impression of noise and laughter. It was happy laughter, not that which would come from meanness or cruel jokes. "By design we operate an open school system. Communications among and between everyone are encouraged," said the principal.

"What you see here is controlled chaos," was how one teacher explained it. "The students are having fun and they are exercising control. If things get out of hand, they settle it and are expected to. We learned in instilling a respect for difference that we had to tolerate some behaviors, speech, or dress that we might not like. It's like flag burning. We had to allow some things that we did not like. We had to give the students control and trust them to use it correctly, as we think they do."

My sense of the place as one of friendliness, with people coming and going freely, fit a parent's description. "This is a good place for young people and for their parents. It makes you feel at home, welcome, and comfortable. It's working class," she continued, "and takes pride in being so. It's a sort of rough and tumble place. Look at the parking lot . . . beat-up cars that the kids, sometimes with their parents, work on and keep going."

CHS was not as clean, neat and orderly as some schools. Student behavior between classes was somewhat loud and chaotic. It was not orderly or, at least, it did not appear orderly to me.

The dress among students was dramatically varied—scruffy, baggy, and loose-fitting, artfully torn here and there. There was nothing elegant about it. And there was a rough and tumble feel to the place that could be off-putting to those who expected schools to be neat and orderly, with authorities always and obviously in control.

To the extent "working class" fit these characteristics, it could apply to CHS. However, it was also the case that many CHS students were the sons and daughters of professionals, small-business owners, and middle managers. Many students were children of teachers in the Cityville system.

"I want my children to know people different from them," said a guidance counselor, "and this is the place to do that. It is also a place where difference is more than tolerated. It is used as a resource here."

Many parents interviewed cited diversity in culture, class, aspirations, and talents as important in their choice of Cityville for their sons and daughters. A set of parents from Cambodia reported in halting English that their son and daughter had spent their freshman years at the Outtown High School. "It was not good. They were laughed at for their sometimes different ways and dress. Not here. Here people are curious because they want to learn about why we came to America and what it was like at home. We feel comfortable here."

Another told me what she and her husband valued about this school. "You should know that [Outtown} high serves a more well-off student body. We actually live close to it and it would have been natural to send our son there. But everyone is very much alike over there. This place is vibrant, and committed to understanding differences. Anyone interested in making their children cosmopolitan will send them here. How can you be educated if you have no ideas, or bad ideas, about people who are different from you. I don't mean just cultural or race differences, but lifestyle too. Also, those who are handicapped . . . our son has MS, but he does very well here. There are many special needs students here. Few are over at the other school."

My sense of the informality and raucous character of the place was reinforced by the multitude of styles of dress. The teacher who spoke of tolerance suggested that the school stretched in terms of what was tolerated. "Some visitors, especially parents, are initially offended. But it seems after a while that most folks aren't bothered. Most say something like they haven't seen so much flesh since they visited the beach."

Diversity in dress was only one dimension of the variety that characterized this school. Cityville was racially and ethnically diverse, with substantial representations of many minorities as well as whites among the student population. Its populations of African-American and Hispanic students were not as great as found in most large city schools. On the other hand, in those large city schools the overwhelming majority of students are African American, often with substantial Hispanic populations. They are usually homogenous in terms of socioeconomic class. Middle and professional class parents in many cities have abandoned city schools for private or suburban schools. Upper class parents have not sent their children in significant numbers to public high schools.

If ethnic, cultural, social, and economic differences among whites are taken into account, CHS was even more diverse. First generation Italian Americans were here; so, too, were Portuguese Americans and Franco-Americans. Add to this mixture the school's substantial African-American, American Indian, and Hispanic populations, combined with the fact that the Asian population was comprised of Vietnamese, Thai, Cambodian, Laotian, and Filipino students, and it became clear the claim of cultural diversity was easily defended.

The principal asserted, "We are predominantly white in terms of number, but we have a lot of racial, ethnic, cultural, and economic differences here."

"It seems," reported one teacher who defended claims about diversity, "that a place has to have all the ingredients of crime and racism to be accepted as 'diverse'. We don't have all those problems, even though we are diverse." Beyond the recognized ethnic groups, "greasers," "preppies," "hoods," and "artists" were social groups recognized and so called at CHS.

"I am sure that you have heard how we try to bring our school's tradition into so many different things in the school," explained a parent. "I am hoping that you also learn about how we use our diversity. It is incorporated in so much that we do. It's why I send my daughter here."

A guidance counselor affirmed this parent's observation and used it as an opportunity to comment at length on the importance of socioeconomic differences in considering Cityville's diverse population.

"We have a large share of students who are technically poor, about 45%. But if you add those on or just a bit above the poverty line, we are probably closer to 55% to 60% poor. We also have some very wealthy kids who are here because their parents like what is here. In between are the middle class kids whose parents are in trades and crafts, or the professions and small businesses. We reflect the city much more than the other high school does. In many ways that is our charm and our strength."

Another guidance counselor was quick to note that the "60% poor or near poor is amazing in terms of our college-bound rates. Our college-bound rate is real testament to our programs and philosophy. Not many schools with our level of poverty send as many kids to colleges as we do. We are proud of that."

Cityville did accommodate its population and turned its diversity into an educational resource. It celebrated difference and built an educational philosophy around it. "By honoring it, we ensure its existence," explained one of the assistant principals. "The cultural and racial differences you see here are here to stay. Before long, people of color will be in the majority in this country, and if we fail to teach everybody that differences are valuable, those of us in the majority today will not have a good time of it in the future."

The curriculum of this school was pervaded by course offerings that reflected the respect for diversity. Special courses in South American and Latin American history were offered. Students were given opportunities to do special research studies directed at cultural diversity, including guided individual and team projects intended to teach them about their cultures and those of others. Language offerings included courses in Chinese, as well as special tutorials in other Asian languages and histories. Individual students were encouraged to report to their fellow students in various ways, including at assemblies, on their ethnic and cultural backgrounds.

The systemic character of Cityville was initially difficult to discern. In fact, it appeared to be unlike schools with a systemic character. The "controlled chaos," as the school's administrator put it (and as its surface suggested), reflected not just a frenetic nature, but a disordered one as well. However, Cityville possessed an essential, systemic, and knowable character. Its basic nature ran throughout and shaped almost everything in the school.

The locus of governance was the "cluster," the primary administrative home for different faculty groups and the academic programs they operated. Clusters, analogous to departments, were based on broad fields of logically and naturally related studies and programs. There was a math/science/industrial arts cluster, an English/foreign language cluster, a health/physical/education cluster, and a history/geography/social studies cluster. "They go back to the 1950s," explained a long time cluster head, "and came about because of the popularity of the broad studies approach that had been trendy in the '40s and '50s and because it was a way of saving money. They seem to be here to stay. And they still probably save us money." The clusters were the strongest, most influential organizational entity in policy and decision making and functioned the way faculty as a whole functioned in some schools.

As depicted in Table 8.1, although CHS was large and seemingly impersonal, it was decentralized, self-consciously and proudly so. Attention to governance and to community building was evident at the decentralized cluster level.

Cityville was something like a college in terms of faculty and governance roles. The cluster and its programs constituted the primary unit of administration and political influence, and collegiality was the basis for personnel decisions, planning, development, and implementation. It was also the basis for the exercise of TPA.

Clusters were also seen as vehicles for humanizing a large school. Although not as large as some big-city schools, Cityville was deemed too large to achieve the intimacy that faculty and administrators felt was necessary to good schooling. According to the head of the math/science/industrial arts cluster, "Bigness is relative. We think 1,200 or so students makes for a large school. A school is supposed to know its students, know them extremely well. The cluster is a way of getting around the impersonality of bigness. We use the cluster to help Cityville be like a small and intimate school."

The fragmentation apparent at Cityville at the overall school level was tempered by the nature and function of clusters, which were centers of community for teachers and students. Each cluster functioned like a community and possessed the culture or ethos of a community, working to build and maintain it.

It was also the case that at Cityville, students were expected to fend for themselves, to become independent and responsible. "I've been at another high school in a suburb of

Table 8.1. The Policy Environment of Cityville Public High School.

MISSION:	*To provide an educational environment that is conducive to realization of individual potentials, and the expression of responsible citizenship, through and with celebration of cultural diversity.*
AMBIENCE:	*A friendly, fast-paced, upbeat, even raucous atmosphere; a sense of majesty and tradition to the building; diversity in all forms is nurtured and celebrated; a user-friendly place.*
ETHOS:	*A pragmatic, driven, individualistic ethic informed by cultural and other sources of diversity evokes a spirit of freedom, pluralism, and self-responsibility.*
GOVERNANCE:	*Hierarchical, formal, and mandated representation at schoolwide level; informal, organic, community-like governance at the powerful cluster level.*
ORGANIZATIONAL CONTROL:	*Arises from the statues and power echelon in schoolwide matters and through informal policy and custom at the cluster level.*
LEADERSHIP:	*Exercised primarily de jure overall. Principal overall leader and authority; cluster heads important and leadership is shared with teachers; all statutory leaders consulted widely and collegially.*
TEACHER PROFESSIONAL AUTHORITY:	*Exercised through representation school wide, collectively at the cluster level; statutes grant teacher voice over broad range of policy and program matters; TPA and autonomy potent.*
SOCIALIZATION:	*Self-conscious at both school and cluster levels; emphasis on conformity at cluster level; cluster philosophy determines practice.*
MORAL AUTHORITY:	*History and renown as urban high school evokes pride; success with diversity makes school attractive and credible to parents and various publics generally; emphasis on the individual is known and generally accepted.*

Boston," claimed a junior, "and it was stodgy and up-tight. This place lets me be and makes me take much more responsibility for myself."

The student captured what several students and teachers had to say. It was no accident that the school functioned this way. It was part of an expressed educational philosophy that appeared in several documents and was invoked in various policy discussions whenever issues arose relative to student behavior or curricular choice. According to the school's "Educational Philosophy" document, Cityville school professionals believed that:

> the development of responsible citizenship is an important part of our curriculum. We promote continued development of moral and ethical values, appreciation for cultural achievements, self responsibility, respect for others, and a sense of individual worth. . . . We encourage independence and responsibility for one's self. . . . The pursuit of opportunity and the attainment of goals is the responsibility of the student.

There did not appear to be anything special in this statement as such. It could have come from many public high schools. However, it combined with policy and practice regarding curriculum, teaching, planning, policymaking, and students to make it consequential for CHS.

Students spoke approvingly of this approach. "I'm glad this place stands for the individual," reported the student who had attended another school outside of Boston. "It is part of becoming educated." Many teachers and parents spoke approvingly, also.

There are some limitations to this individualistic ethic. Some were expressed by a guidance counselor. "Taking charge of one's life and making choices is what being an adult is all about. But heaven knows how poorly many of us do with this part of adulthood. Why should we expect more of teenagers? Even those students who think it's great for them are not ready for this freedom and responsibility. They need much more adult prescription in their lives. They need more of being told what to do. [Cityville] has a different view."

Other school professionals acknowledged the need to continually think about the possible negative consequences of their school's philosophy, but they agreed overall with the sentiments expressed by a school board member. "We have a good track record with what Cityville school has been doing. It shouldn't be messed over with constant change. Don't fix what ain't broke, as the saying goes."

The ethos of Cityville was indicated by its ambient "loose-ness," its tolerance of a wide range of dress and behavior from students, its decentralized approach to a great deal of policy and decision making, and by its emphasis on independence, individual worth, and responsibility. The focus on individualism was, however, tempered. Diversity in many forms, including cultural diversity, was respected, appreciated, celebrated, and employed as an educational resource. To this extent, roots and belonging were prized and reinforced. Further, values at the cluster level revealed a concern for community. Within clusters, community, belonging, and conformity were valued. On the other hand, autonomy was highly valued at the schoolwide level.

Given the complex, somewhat confusing and chaotic messages about diversity and community, I did not initially expect to find either of these concepts clearly or consistently articulated in the school's statement of purpose. I learned otherwise.

Documents that addressed purpose were remarkably consistent, as were answers to questions I raised about it. The mission statement was broad enough to allow for cluster expressions of uniqueness of purpose, and it granted endorsement of an overall school and cluster approach that cultivated and valued differences. The commonly expressed, widely agreed on mission of Cityville was to "provide an educational environment conducive to the realization of individual potentials and to the expression of responsible citizenship through and with celebration of cultural diversity." This mission statement appeared in various CHS publications and documents, including those widely distributed to students and parents. It was known to and reported as appropriate by everyone I encountered. "Of course, we know about it. After all, what would you expect?" asked a parent. "We chose this place, and we did so only after learning what it was like. Do you know anyone these days who sends their children to a city school without knowing about that school, if they don't have to send their kids there?"

Purpose expressed within the clusters tended to be personalistic and nurturing. This reflected accommodations in Cityville's policy environment. Most such compromises, "some intentional," according to the principal, protected against the emergence of too strong an individualistic ethic against a compulsively conformist one.

A connection between the school's ambience and its mission was manifest. Queries about which came first, the stated purpose or the culture of diversity, brought smiles. "It is hard to figure out," replied a chemistry teacher. "We hadn't thought much about this particular question until you asked it last time you were here. I understand that if you want to know why a successful school is successful, you will want to know something about how it got that way. But we haven't spent too much time thinking about that."

Another teacher pointed out that, "Differences among students have been clear during the 15 years I've been around. Our philosophy statement and policies probably came second." Others confirmed this teacher's report. A teacher of French observed, "You can't have a school serving city kids and not have pluralism. So we took what we had. Then we worked at knowing what we believed in, expressed those beliefs, and saw them through in decisions about programs, discipline, and so on."

This observation prompted a teacher of Spanish to point out, "We got a vision of what we should be, and we got consensus around it. We asked ourselves things like 'what kinds of things are we doing to fulfill this vision?', 'what kinds of things are in the way of helping us get to it?'"

"There are the obvious reasons why we use our mix as an educational opportunity," explained a school board member, "but above all else it is to make sure that as many students as possible get a chance to succeed. [CHS] staff were convinced long ago that differences in experience, probably especially those rooted in culture, produce different strengths and capacities. We want to tap into these, and we have evidence here that building on diversity does it."

Cityville was also proud of the diverse student "stars" it produced. It graduated its fair share of winners of academic prizes and awards, but it was also proud of its special athletes, drama students, and artists. It was able to raise and distribute over $50,000 in academic and other scholarships and awards for its last graduation ceremony.

Although faculty and others were initially taken aback with my questions about the origins and order of their mission and related school characteristics, they evinced general agreement. They had not been reflective about the steps that brought them to their current state. So, initially they had to grope for answers. Nevertheless, there was virtual unanimity among all queried that a crisis and a strong response from the superintendent were the prime movers in these developments, followed by a faculty that took responsibility for the school and a principal that went along.

Reports tended to merge with that offered by a long-time veteran math teacher who spoke for others in telling the following story.

"We were in the pits. The local press and the state department of education were all over our backs for a combination of things. The newspaper published a story about several years of very poor student performance on testing. We had many dropouts. A student was injured in a fight on the school grounds. It all brought us down. A special meeting was called by the superintendent, and he made it clear that we had better change or some drastic steps would be taken. To this day I don't know what those steps would have been, but we set up a task force that worked over a Spring and a Summer, surveying everyone in the school. The task force eventually came up with a statement of beliefs and an educational philosophy that we adopted and have updated over the years. The administrations of the school have participated in these efforts and supported them, and we refer to these beliefs and philosophy whenever an issue comes up and a decision has to be made. All this started 11 years ago. And things seemed to develop from all that."

Teachers also tended to agree that these early, crisis-induced initiatives were the beginning of teacher pride in and commitment to a major role for them in policy and decision making. They were the beginning of the important place of the cluster in insuring teachers a central place in power and decision making in the school.

"The cluster was here before the superintendent told us to shape up or ship out, but it wasn't as important as it is now," reported a cluster head. "It existed then to show an organizational chart of where people and programs belonged." That early role was a far cry from the centrality to which the cluster system evolved.

The relationship of the mission to the curriculum was also evident. The range of curricular offerings was broad; the terrain it covered was expansive, but not just in terms of academic or scholarly subjects. Courses were offered in the performing and fine arts, and in arts and crafts. There were several courses in creative writing, a few on film making, a respectable array of courses in the traditional academic subjects, and, as already noted, numerous special offerings relative to diversity.

The concern for diversity and the pervading philosophy of individual responsibility were echoed in the expression of teacher professional authority at Cityville. TPA was exercised most visibly within the clusters. Each cluster was a miniature community in which members exercised authority broadly, in depth, and consequentially. They did so collaboratively, as well. In the clusters, issues were heard in a town meeting fashion. Problems were addressed by all the members, and plans for the future were shaped in the light of input from everyone who wished to provide it. If decisions made affected only the cluster, they were then finalized and acted on with no external help or interference. "Our clusters run everything," reported a cluster head. "They have become the centerpieces of this place."

TPA was also visible at the schoolwide level. Faculty and staff from the clusters and from service units were elected, or volunteered to serve on schoolwide committees and task forces. Such representation was a matter of official policy and of teacher union contract agreements.

"We have a major voice over school matters through these assignments, but we usually bring a lot of discussion from the cluster level," explained the chair of the school's curriculum development committee. The extent and importance of the discussion the teacher referred to depended on the degree of importance and on any controversy associated with issues and tasks.

"Typically," said a teacher who served on many schoolwide committees, "the day-to-day business of these committees doesn't get us very excited as a group so we just go about our business. But I am expected to represent my cluster in those committees and I'd better not let something slip by me." Indeed, this person's membership on so many committees was explained by another as due to the fact that "she has a reputation for being serious and professional about this business. She is known as quite able in taking care of our interests. That is important to us."

Formal policy with respect to TPA was stated officially as follows in the *Teachers Handbook*:

> Because it is considered essential to sound policy making, teacher input in decisions is consistently sought. The formal vehicles for teacher participation include regularly scheduled cluster meetings, curriculum subcommittee meetings, faculty-administrative liaison committee meetings, and service on ad hoc committees and task forces as needed.

The attitude of the central administration toward each cluster and toward teachers in the classroom was laissez-faire. Each organizational layer and each individual seemed comfortable minding only their own "store," and seemed to feel others could be trusted. The consequence was a great deal of autonomy in the classroom in the overall context of the school. That autonomy was jealously protected by custom and by teacher union contract.

"I taught at a community college for a year during a leave of absence once," explained a teacher of math. "And I felt right at home the way the math department and others operated over there and the way our cluster works here."

On the other hand, teacher autonomy in the context of the cluster was another matter. The cluster groupings of math/science/industrial arts and of English/foreign language insisted that new teachers, whether new to teaching or new to the Cityville system, receive orientations to the cluster and to that cluster's favored approaches to teaching, dealing with students, and teacher evaluations.

"We expect our views to be expressed when these people are being recruited," reported the chair of one of the clusters. "Recruits are screened accordingly. But that doesn't always happen. Even when it does, it doesn't always 'take', so we have this orientation. We also insist that our supervisors work with the rookies to ensure compliance to the extent possible with our approach. All of us discuss this at cluster meetings, and as a supervisor I am expected to insist that even old-timers follow our system."

The cluster head at Cityville was first among equals. Custom and tradition internal to the cluster prevailed in decisions and in day-to-day operations. The socialization of newcomers and the maintenance of the membership of all was important. Thus, each cluster was more or less conformist. A strong sense of shared purpose prevailed, and loyalties to the cluster were expected. Newcomers and veterans received ongoing socialization.

It appeared that the socialization for newcomers and for veterans had indirectly influenced the principal. Relatively new to the position, she came from outside the system. She had been a teacher within Cityville's school system, then a special education coordinator at the central administration level, then an assistant superintendent of instruction in a large midwestern school system. She had been back at Cityville for two years.

"I knew I had made a mistake within weeks of leaving this city some ten years ago," she reported, "and when the principal's job became available I worked hard to get a crack at it. I am thankful that I did."

A teacher reported that the principal "has been smart enough so far not to mess up the cluster arrangement and its role in governance and everything else." The principal acknowledged that she was not interested in making changes in clusters. "I have my reservations about some aspects of the clusters, but they tend not to be about governance. In time, I may try to make some administrative moves on those concerns, but not for a while. I am still learning my job, but from what I can tell, the cluster arrangement serves this place very well."

The principal was assertive and took her statutory power

quite seriously. She was interested, as she put it at a general faculty meeting, "in eliminating the weaknesses of CHS and in maximizing the strengths. Lack of overall, schoolwide leadership has been a great weakness; I will work to overcome that. The cluster organization is a major strength."

This is not to suggest that Cityville was a balkanized state. The "school," through the principal and standing committees, was an important arbiter of direction and policy. The role of data-based planning at Cityville is illustrative.

For several years the school had been building an expanding bank of databases that served to drive selected schoolwide and cluster policies and practices. I observed several school-wide standing committee meetings at which administrators and faculty representatives reported developments in regard to various data. I witnessed reports that included data on the average daily attendance of students and teachers, student performance on statewide and nationally normed achievement tests, attendance at football games, extracurricular participation rates, grade distributions, and booster club funds raised. In each instance, the person reporting included previous years' data and outcomes, targets that had been set for the current year, and progress toward those targets. In several instances wall charts were used to report on these matters, and the charts were later hung in the halls or in a classroom.

In some cases, teachers, along with administrators, parents, and students, worked together to realize the target goals. The principal observed that one could get the "impression that Cityville is simply a holding company for clusters. The data-based planning and targets show otherwise, and contribute to a schoolwide culture."

Leadership was exercised by the principal from both a human relations dimension and from the context of position power. The place of the clusters and cluster heads in the system ensured wider leadership involvement than would otherwise be the case.

Clusters came into their place of authority, at least in the early years, in a de facto manner. The superintendent expressed it this way: "We need strong clusters and strong cluster heads because principals come and go. Our current principal has been here for two years, and it looks like she might stay a while. But before her we had one that was acting for two years, another that stayed for only two, and two previous others that served only a year each. If this place is good and successful it is because of the leadership of cluster heads and of the quality of the clusters."

The moral authority of Cityville was derived from its success with a diverse student body, its exceptional record in sending a high number of its graduates to colleges, and its success in placing its graduates in good jobs.

The school emphasized the practical value of the diploma as a credential. The clusters, however, fleshed out and embellished this value and its meaning. Each cluster worked in developing the loyalties and natural regard of its students and professionals.

"We take advantage of the bragging rights our record gives us," explained a cluster head, "and we do it all the time so that this city and those that run it know how good we are. We don't need them trying to fix us all the time like other city schools. We do our job better than most and that is what we market to the city."

The moral authority of the school per se was derived from its success through its clusters. A situation I encountered involving some of Cityville's students may be revealing. Shortly after I began my in-depth visit to Cityville, I found myself looking out a third floor hallway window to a small neighborhood grocery and deli across the street. Students were going in and out of the place, for sandwiches and sodas, I assumed. I was struck by all the activity around the store.

A couple of days after my initial observations of the store, I noticed that students were usually not coming out with sandwiches or sodas and that those frequenting the place seemed to be alike in terms of dress. Occasionally, cars would pull up in front of the store, double park, someone would run in and out, and then drive off.

A couple of days later yet, I saw two adults staring at the store from the school's second floor windows. I joined them, assuming they were faculty members I had not met. "What goes on over there?", I asked after introducing myself.

"Drugs," said the one I had thought might be a coach, "not hard stuff—pot, hash, pills."

"Doesn't anyone do anything about it?", I asked.

" That's why we're here," replied the scholarly looking one. "We're checking to see if a delivery is made to the store."

These were not teachers or coaches. They were narcotics detectives with the Cityville police. I learned that they came to the school every now and then, and made an arrest every now and then, but they and the school authorities had not been successful at stemming the flow of these drugs. The school was more or less resigned to the limits of its power. It urged students not to frequent the store and occasionally threatened suspension, but did not press what "it learned it couldn't do much about or might only make worse," reported a teacher.

"The fact is that there is not much that we can do," said a guidance counselor.

This laissez-faire perspective was expressed by others and contrasted with what would be the case at many schools. Some schools would view themselves as moral authorities obligated to do something, even if it was ineffectual. Cityville felt that its limited resources demanded that it invest its moral authority in that which paid dividends, although some teachers and cluster heads suggested that more assertive action would be taken if the clusters were the points of decision and action in this matter.

"Maybe it's because we know the students better than those in the principal's and central offices. Maybe because we are accustomed to taking action at this level here at [Cityville]. But the way administrators and central administration have dealt with this is in keeping with this school's overall emphasis on kids as decision makers."

Cityville's perspective on students who frequented the grocery store was consistent with its overall philosophy. It is conceivable that the institution could take a different position on this issue without violating their creed, but they did not. "Even if we are wrong on this one, and there are days when I think we are," said one of the assistant principals who listened to the earlier-quoted guidance counselor who had bemoaned the amount of freedom students were given, "I think in the long haul we serve our students better if we stick to our customary way. It's their life, they have to learn to live it."

This assistant principal expressed what so many did at Cityville and at the other schools; that a proven educational philosophy must be adhered to even though some students may not be served by it. Observed a teacher at one of the schools, "The fact is that a public school cannot be everything to everybody. It can be very important to the great majority of students, but only if it is consistent. Sticking with a philosophy that makes clear what policy and practice to follow is necessary to serve that majority." There was every indication that the majority of Cityville's students were indeed well served.

Postscript

Two findings account for what is most compelling about the effective schools literature. They are:

1. school characteristics can have positive effects on the academic performance of students who are poor
2. successful schools share common traits

The first finding challenged the most disturbing conclusions of Coleman et al. (1966), Jencks et al. (1972), and other studies of the effects of schooling; the second study led to countless initiatives to impel all schools to adopt traits seen as common to effective schools.

The three schools in this study possess many traits attributed to effective schools. However, this study went beyond confirming the existence of those traits; much of that task was accomplished in the SSRP process. This study focused on the *policy environments* of three "good enough" high schools (see Chapter 3) that were unique to each school. These policy environments were comprised of policy elements that existed in each school, but were unique in their expression. The important point here is that school reform through incorporation or emulation of the traits of successful schools, or even merely successful practices, cannot be accomplished wholesale without attention to the unique policy environments and constituent policy elements within each school. With that in mind, this postscript is intended to highlight the policy elements, comparing how they were manifested in the different schools.

POLICY ELEMENTS

Mission

Each school in this study had a compelling, unique mission that had been fashioned with broad participation that reflected the communities served by the school. These missions shaped and were shaped by other building-level policy elements.

Ruraldom's mission reflected and drove its commitment to satisfy the social-psychological and academic needs of students from its economically depressed communities. Townston maximized the ambitions of upwardly mobile parents to promote academic achievement. Cityville used cultural and other sources of diversity to promote realization of individual potential, respect for diversity, and responsible citizenship.

The significance of these missions lay in the way they functioned and their relations to other salient policy elements. Specifically, each

- reflected the populations served
- served to marshall resources
- articulated school professionals' responsibilities
- served as a standard against which decisions were evaluated

The mission of each school was reflected in, reinforced by, and reinforcing of other policy elements.

We learned from these successful schools that mission was not simply a vision of what a school was supposed to be. It was normative, a directing and regulating force, and it was chosen.

Teacher Professional Authority

What first captured my attention about these schools was the unusually high degree of teacher professional authority in all of them. Teachers exercised a voice in building-level philosophy, decision making, and policy making seldom seen in American public schools. Early in my study I observed that TPA was exercised differently from school to school, which gave rise to the policy environment orientation of the study. TPA opened up additional learning as well.

Most public school teachers in this country have little TPA. Reasons for this vary, but it may be due in part to the fact that high TPA does not guarantee reduction in other assignments, nor does it bring higher salaries. High TPA means high workload. A teacher at a school I visited for the SSRP remarked, "a teacher who wants a lot of policy and decision authority *deserves* it."

Teachers did not receive release time for their TPA. They had on average seven assigned periods a day, five classes to teach (with an average of three different preparations), one preparation period, one supervisory period, and 22 minutes for lunch, often with concurrent supervisory responsibilities. Thus, teachers in the schools had teaching and related assigned workloads comparable to those of high school teachers across the country. Their TPA brought them many additional responsibilities.

The professional commitment and demanding workload of teachers in these schools, like the policy environments themselves, were a function of choice. Teachers grumbled from time to time; they expressed frustration and fatigue; the quality of their family life suffered. Nonetheless, they exercised a major voice in the making of their roles. And as the narratives made clear, these teachers preferred this voice to what they experienced in other, less demanding schools. Perhaps the principals who were present at RUHS and TRHS when crises shook these schools were indispensable to the schools' ultimate success. However, it was teachers with professional authority who were necessary over the long term to ensure continuing success.

I cannot imagine any of these schools being what they were and functioning as they did without high TPA. I can imagine them without their principals. Indeed, the successful CHS functioned superbly in the wake of some mobility among its principals. In short, TPA was the most distinctive feature of leadership in these schools.

Governance and Leadership

Human relations, leadership, and governance patterns in each school reflected the unique ambience and ethos of each. This uniqueness made for different roles for all concerned, including the principal. At RUHS, he was first among equals, whereas the principal at TRHS was the first, albeit with very strong departments and departmental chairpersons. At CHS the cluster heads were first among equals at that level and exercised a great deal of authority at the school level. The CHS principal's leadership derived from statutory authority and was acknowledged by all, including the current principal, as "constrained" in the face of and compared to the collective leadership of cluster heads and teachers.

Effective schools researchers unanimously claim that schools become effective as a result of being led to effectiveness. Further, they see leadership by the principal as the necessary condition in this regard. Ronald Edmonds (in Squires, Huitt, & Segars, 1983) put it this way: "There are some bad schools with good principals but there are no good schools with bad principals."

The principals in the schools in this study were important to their schools' success. They recognized what the teachers and students were capable of achieving; they expected high achievement and strong performance; they gave a great deal of support and understanding to help all to meet those expectations. Each was sufficiently secure to support high TPA. Each could have been an obstacle to their school's success, but they were competent and smart administrators who knew in part when to stay out of the way.

A unitary prescription, then, for how a principal should lead for an effective or successful school is off base. In fact, a case could be made that the emphasis on the principal in the effective schools research literature reinforced the excessive statutory authority of principals, promoting an unproductive absence of attention to the place of teachers as school policymakers.

Ethos

All three schools were infused with prevailing values and beliefs that were often invoked in accounting for policies and practice. This ethos was evident to me and to others in the overall atmosphere of the schools, in the relations among people in them, in the way school professionals worked for their schools' and students' success, and in many other ways. The principal at Ruraldom illuminated the importance and potency of an underlying ethos when he told me, "People in this school believe that public schooling exists to give all kids a fair shot at social opportunity and success. That is what we are all about. We believe in this; it is the basis for all that we do."

Ruraldom school professionals believed that a "fair shot" for their students demanded a caring and supportive ethos. So they treated students lovingly, promoted a sense of community and belonging, and stressed individual and collective benefits of hard work. The communitarian ethos of RUHS contrasted sharply with the individualistic, competitive ethos of TRHS, and with the individual freedom and responsibility, laissez-faire ethos, of CHS.

It is important to note, again, that the ethos of each school was chosen. These were not accidents loosely linked to other normative features and values of the school. They were the results of discussions, sometimes heated debates, and decisions.

The more the beliefs and principles that create an ethos are known and expressed, the more they and the ethos become embedded in the policy fabric of the schools and in the thoughts and behaviors of those in them. To know that in terms of dominant character or policy environment one school is communitarian, another is business-like and intolerant of sloth, and another is informal and loosely structured is to have a sense of each school. We could predict what the ambience of each would be, and what it would be like for teachers and students in it. To know this is to begin to know and to be able to predict what is demanded of students and school professionals, what kinds of governance patterns and organizational control exist, and whether one would like to be a student or a professional in that school, or to have children who attend it.

Ambience

Each school had a distinct, strongly-felt, consciously created "feeling" or atmosphere. Effective schools literature might refer to this as a "school climate." I have called it *ambience* for reasons discussed in Chapter 5.

The ambience of each school was made, at least in part, by school professionals' decisions about how they wanted their schools to "feel," as the principal of Cityville put it. "We wanted our regulations about student behavior in the hallways to suggest what this place values. We wanted parents and visitors to know what we feel about differences among people. People can pick that up by what they see in how students dress, and the ways students come and go," she concluded. Thus, ambience at CHS, as in the other schools, was expressed in, reinforced by, and reinforcing of other elements in the policy environment.

Perhaps there is nothing surprising in the observation that a school with a mission of, for example, promoting students' achievement through social and emotional as well as academic nurturance, would also be characterized by an ambience of caring and warmth. However, it appears from this study that this inter-dependency among policy elements is the case only if each element is more than words on a document and is directive of values and behaviors of professionals and students in a school. Consistency among elements was evident in ways both trivial and profound, from the signs and symbols in the hallways, to the relationships among people.

The ambience of these schools was strongly felt because it was communicated powerfully: in the way people related to one another, in the cleanliness of the buildings and grounds, in the ways halls and walls were used, and in the pride expressed about the school. All these, again, did not just happen. They reflected decisions about ways of being that, in turn, affected more specific decisions, such as what could be posted on the walls, or rules and regulations regarding leaving classrooms.

Each school in this study, although ordered and disciplined, and explicit about rules and punishment for rules broken, eschewed policies and practices that might discomfort or estrange. School professionals worked to avoid suspensions and disciplinary action and to keep their students out of trouble. Each of these schools adopted (at the school-level at RUHS, and primarily at the cluster and department levels at CHS and TRHS) a student-centered approach often associated with elementary schools. These schools extended the individualized and nurturing ambience of the elementary school into the high school.

Socialization

In most schools in the United States, teachers learn they have new colleagues on the first day of the school year. Further, even with teacher orientation programs, most schools slight the socialization of teachers to their particular social system. As in so many other ways, the schools in this study were different. The recruitment, hiring, and development of faculty and other school professionals were not taken for granted or left to administrators.

Socialization was very important to the schools in this study. School professionals believed new teachers needed help to succeed, and they developed structured ways to give that help.

Socialization also was used for a more systemic purpose than insuring success of individual new teachers. School professionals sought also to maintain their social systems; socialization was a necessary condition for doing so. Socialization ensured that newcomers got acclimated and learned to accommodate to established ways, and it helped veterans remain committed to these ways.

At Ruraldom, socialization generated what I perceived as conformity, a characteristic uncomfortable for me and offensive to some observers. Professionals at Ruraldom were quick to note that they "see it as a professional responsibility to let potential employees know as much as possible about what they are going to get into at this school." One RUHS teacher spoke for her colleagues when she said, "If we're too conforming, so be it. It works for us. If people don't like it or can't hack it, the door is not locked. They can move on."

Townston and Cityville socialized at the cluster and department levels as RUHS did at the school level. They sought to ensure that the values, cultures, and functioning of departments and clusters were instilled in newcomers and maintained by veterans. At Townston and Cityville they appeared to be less concerned with these matters at the school level because they believed the local unit, department and cluster, respectively, was the basis of community.

Teachers have long been taught to employ their unique personalities and styles of teaching; administrators have been taught to protect individuality and to maximize individual strengths. In the schools I studied, however, the converse often seemed to be the case. In these schools, especially at RUHS, professionals worked to ensure that newcomers were socialized into their uniformities; those who could not or would not adjust were marginalized very quickly, in the hope that they would choose to leave.

I sought earlier (Chapter 3) to make clear that when I used the term "good" to describe the schools in this study, I was revealing the influence of Lightfoot's notion of the "good enough" school; also, I had in mind certain qualities associated with performance and success, rather than moral or aesthetic ones. I was thinking of the conforming aspects of RUHS when I was trying to make this point. I found those aspects of RUHS—and others in the other schools—distasteful, not to my liking, and lacking in aesthetic "goodness."

Moral Authority

Professionals in the schools in this study attributed their success over time to effective socialization of faculty, staff, and students, and to the philosophies and values of their schools. The success of socialization and educational philosophy allowed them to enjoy a high degree of moral authority with the different publics to which they were accountable. In fact, even though all of these schools enjoyed excellent school-parent and school-community relations, and even though Ruraldom, especially, had parents and members of the community heavily involved with the schools, none of these schools had much intervention or "interference" from parents or others in educational matters. The schools were the source, rather than the receiver, of the community's educational moral voice.

Something I witnessed enlightened me about how strongly some felt about leaving "well enough alone" in these schools. I had the opportunity to observe a board of education interview session with a candidate for the superintendency of one of the school systems in this study. The candidate was told by several of the interviewers that if he were selected he would be expected to "leave . . . [Ruraldom] be. They are doing just fine and don't need to be led from the central office." I became convinced this attitude was widely shared among members of the community, suggesting one reason why parent involvement typically supported the school rather than influenced it.

I do not mean to suggest that parents and communities were given short shrift by the subject schools. On the contrary, each of these schools had intentional systems that reflected the needs and demands of their clients. In each case it appeared that the constituents had been satisfied. The schools offered missions shaped by the school professionals' view of the nature and needs of their students and communities. They delivered on the promises of their missions in ways that satisfied. And parents and the communities seemed to say that as long as they were satisfied, they would leave the schools alone except to help when requested.

All the subject schools worked to ensure maintenance of a positive ambience. All of them communicated widely to broadcast good news. "I remember going through my mail and finding a letter from the principal," reported a Townston parent. "My heart jumped a beat. I was sure something was wrong with Chuck at school. I opened the envelope to find a very short note. It said, 'Dear Mr. & Mrs. [Coates], I saw Chuck help out one of our handicapped students today. He carried the student to a class after an armrest on the wheelchair came apart. Chuck did this quietly, without fanfare and attention. Congratulations for such a fine young man.' I tell you. I was higher than a kite for a long time."

The principal who authored this note told me that he tried to set aside about 15 minutes every day to write what he called "good news notes." They went to parents, students, teachers, newspaper reporters, assistant principals, central staff and administrators, and many others. The principal would make a note to himself whenever he saw or heard of some good deed, good performance, or something that he believed was good for the school. "I guess I average five or six notes a week," he said. That works out to be quite a few notes over a short period of time."

Other principals and school professionals among the three schools had their own regular means of writing up and reporting individual and collective success stories. But all did something like this. As a consequence, all enjoyed extremely positive relations with local media and with parents and community leaders. People in the communities were very well-informed about the positive side of these schools. The schools and school professionals, in turn, got enormous mileage out of these communication patterns.

I have worked to show, then, that all the policy elements identified in this study were present at each school. Although different in form in different schools, they served similar functions. When taken together, they constituted vastly different policy environments, demonstrating how difficult and ineffective it would be to mandate for these schools any specific reform.

The other important point is that these profoundly different schools would all be deemed successful by almost any criteria. It is by charting the individual policy elements of the schools that we come to understand their success as an outcome of elegant internal consistency.

Beyond all of the promises and constraints evident in these schools, the overpowering feature of each was uniqueness. Each school had a "personality," an identity that was singular. This unique identity was partly a consequence of obvious and oft-cited demographics: the number of students served, individual school histories, political factors, cultural and socioeconomic populations served, and other context shaping forces. However, the subject schools were unique in other and seemingly more important ways as well. Consider the ways each policy element was rendered unique in nature and function within a given school. Each school had a mission, each had a strongly felt ethos, for example. But

each of these policy elements and the others were unique not simply of themselves, but because of the way they functioned in the
context of each school's policy environment. This is important in
fully understanding a school and in understanding school effectiveness and school reform.

Part III

The Policy Environment Perspective

Chapter 9

The Paradox

All American public schools are the same; each American public school is unique (Tye, 1987).

This paradox has intrigued educational researchers. Tye (1987) tells us that knowing how a school is unique and how it is like all others can inform change strategy. This makes sense, but the policy environments of the schools of this study suggest that it is important to be explicit and inclusive in looking at the dimensions of sameness and difference. We need to know how these dimensions interact and whether they are internally consistent. The policy environment perspective holds that understanding a school's policy elements and their interaction clarifies uniqueness, leads to finding indicators of a school's readiness for change, and illuminates points of access at which change may be effectively introduced.

Uniformity among schools is comparatively easy to locate. It can be found in what Tye (1987) called the "deep structures of schooling" (p. 282) and what Goodlad (1984) called the "enduring mechanics of curriculum, didactics, or age-graded instruction." (p. 299). Both have in mind that school days are characteristically fragmented into six to eight time frames of about 35

133

to 55 minutes, classrooms are physically arranged in relatively few different configurations, program curricula are remarkably similar across the country, teacher talk dominates in classrooms, relatively few textbooks are marketed and distributed nationally, curriculum is structured in a lock-step grade and age pattern, students are tested and graded in only a few ways, and local, state, and federal laws and policies are similar in their impact on the nature and function of American public schools.

Often disparaged as dreary conformity, school sameness is generally regarded as an understandable outcome of potent, sometimes necessary, external standardizing forces. This is especially true with regard to matters of equality of opportunity, as "equality" implies sameness of condition and treatment.

Traits on which schools are alike are those that are more amenable to measurement. So it is factors which are uniform that become the basis on which large-scale school improvement initiatives are framed. Inasmuch as schools are alike, it makes sense to assume they are comparably susceptible to change through similar means (Tye, 1987). However, all schools are also unique.

Although schools may be similar to one another, it is equally true that they are profoundly different. Anyone who has been a student in or who has taught in different schools has experienced such difference. The narratives in Part II point to the uniqueness of three particular schools. Deeper study (see Chapters 10 and 11) makes clear that the mere possession of policy elements that are similar in nature is not sufficient to render schools comparable. For example, many schools are alike in having a widely understood and compelling mission. However, the nature of the mission varies from school to school. Consider the differences in mission among the subject schools (see Tables 6.1, 7.1, and 8.1). Moreover, the manner in which missions function, given other policy elements within a school, will vary from school to school, also contributing to a school's uniqueness. The interaction between sameness and uniqueness is thus fundamental to knowing something about a school, its readiness for change and reform generally, and its accessibility to certain kinds of change in particular. For example, to introduce a change in ethos in Townston Regional High School without attention to Townston's mission, its governance, its TPA, or its moral authority with its particular publics would be to court failure.

Although school sameness is often seen as a necessary evil, school uniqueness is typically regarded as an expression of a vital pluralism, a consequence of cherished local control. Uniqueness in schools is seen as the domain into which one could infuse, and from which could be derived, creative policies and practices. Uniqueness is also valued because characteristics associated with it are among those aspects of schools thought to be most consequential.

Nevertheless, uniqueness has received comparatively little attention in educational research and policy studies. This is due in part to the fact that uniqueness, usually attributable to intangible factors, is difficult to measure and manipulate. It is not susceptible to the kinds of statistical treatments and comparative analyses so frequently applied to conditions that are uniform in schools. Also, studies of schools' uniqueness do not occasion broad generalizations that can lead to widespread applications.

Coming to know and appreciate uniqueness requires labor-intensive, costly study. Consequently, those aspects of schools with which uniqueness is associated are usually addressed in terms of external school-shaping forces (e.g., history, geopolitical setting, demographics, idiosyncratic community needs and demands); the distinctiveness of these is obvious. In this way, school individuality per se is granted, but it remains ambiguous; a school's singularity becomes merely an extension of its situation and remains abstract.

Studies intended to understand and explain a school's unique character have usually been anthropological in character and ethnographic in method (e.g., Cusick, 1983; Grant, 1988; Lightfoot, 1983; Metz, 1986). They have been designed to reveal the nature of the school from the inside, through observations and recordings of researchers. Such studies are illuminating. They have, though, been confined, limited in generalizability, and too idiosyncratic and expensive for replicable, broad-scale studies. We then confront this dilemma: We want school reform to occur within the context of a school's uniqueness. The policy environment perspective indicates that it must. Understanding a school's uniqueness reveals a school's potential for change generally, the kind of change it can accommodate, and the access points for change. Conversely, it is by virtue of uniqueness that a school may be impervious to real change. Such understanding, however costly and limited, is necessary if we want change and reform.

Mandates for broad reform, especially popular since the publication of *A Nation At Risk* in 1983, of necessity slight and often assault schools' uniqueness. Further, such efforts at change put good schools at risk; characteristics of schools that are correlated with success are vulnerable to mutation or erosion if subjected to commanded reform. The irreconcilability of school individuality with externally mandated change condemns most "outside" reform to failure.

This is not the case with all mandated change. Cuban (1990) has observed that since the turn of the century changes that have been incorporated into the schools have generally been of the large commanded sort. He calls them "first order changes" that try to make what already exists more efficient and effective without substantially changing the way in which teachers, other school professionals, and children perform.

Examples of Cuban's first order changes include the National Defense Education Act of 1958, the Elementary and Secondary Education Act of 1965, and the Education for All Handicapped Children Act of 1975 (Cuban, 1990). These acts produced a number of changes—new specializations, new physical facilities, new programs, new classification systems, and expanded testing. These are the kinds of changes that acknowledge schools' sameness and their capacity to accommodate such changes. They are primarily changes in "deep structures" or "enduring mechanics" rather than in things that make schools unique. Accordingly, they have not wrought the promised dramatic revolutions. "[T]he promise of educational reform as a means of improving teaching and learning has yet to be realized," according to Elmore and McLaughlin (1988) in their comprehensive study of reform effects. They conclude:

> In this pessimistic sense, educational reform is "steady work." That is, the rewards are puny, measured by . . . changes in what is taught and how; but the work is steady, because there is a limitless supply of new ideas for how schools should be changed and no shortage of political and social pressure to force those ideas onto the political agenda. (p. 3)

The lessons of externally mandated reform efforts over the years suggest that certain kinds of change can be made by external command, but those have a narrow effect on what goes on in the day-to-day business of the school. The task at hand, then, is for those who know schools to find new ways to see them, so that the richness of their differences can be embraced with the same alacrity as the safety of their sameness. Only then will our study of schools be informed by what is, instead of by what is convenient. Only such informed study can point us to methods of reform that yield schools not just changed but genuinely improved as places to teach and learn.

Chapter 10

The Logic of the Policy Environment

Policy environment is my construct for the totality of what the school professionals I studied made of their schools. It was not a part of their lexicon or consciousness. Aspects of a school's policy environment came to the attention of these professionals as features of their work world when issues and problems arose, or when policy decisions were being considered. For example, in discussions of a proposed induction program for new teachers, a group of professionals at Cityville raised questions about the program relative to the school's overall goals and its governance patterns. At Ruraldom, a proposal for setting aside an area for student smoking gave rise to heated discussion about matters of ambience and ethos, although these were not the terms used by the discussants. It was, then, issues related in some way to professional domains and to beliefs and fundamental values reflected in school policies and practices that brought attention to the policy environment.

In each school depicted in this study, the policy environment, or aspects of it would be evoked as people made all of those decisions necessary to create and maintain their school. In this sense, policy elements of each policy environment arose self-consciously; of course, without use of those terms. Ruraldom, for example, was self-conscious about its community maintenance (its *ambience*), its support for students (its *ethos*), and the place of a teacher voice (*teacher professional authority*) in its decision making. The emphasis on these and other policy matters reflected educational values, beliefs, and commitments that these school professionals debated and shaped into policy. They and others close to the school could explain why things were as they were at RUHS. This was also the case with the other two schools.

When asked how their schools got that way, school professionals could not answer easily. They revealed a lack of reflection about the evolutionary development of their school's character. Most could point back a few years to some crisis that was a turning point in their school's history. The nature of the crisis (different for each school), the suggested solution and means to reach it, and perhaps the perceived magnitude of the problem as well, had moved the actors to consensus. All involved agreed that unusual measures were necessary; these included more building-level authority and flexibility. Indeed, the comparatively high TPA in all of these schools appeared to be one byproduct of those days of crisis. Perhaps this was also true relative to other unique features of the schools—Ruraldom's social service mission, for example. That is, crisis provided opportunity for different, if not radical, approaches.

Whether or not it was a crisis that moved the schools to efficacy or success, there was a discernible logic to their policy environments, a coherence among the policy elements, and an integrity to the policy environment that, I have inferred, may be lacking in less successful schools.

All schools, I believe, have a policy environment; all policy environments have policy elements. All policy environments, as policy environments, have certain characteristics. The three schools of this study demonstrate that the policy environments of successful or "good enough" schools have certain features that may distinguish them from the policy environments of less successful schools.

In this chapter I describe the characteristics of policy environments that are shared by the schools of this study. These characteristics communicate a great deal about the nature and operations of these schools, about the potential of each for change, about what kind of change might be most appropriate for each, and about where and how best to initiate change. Before turning to them, however, some cautionary points need attention.

I noted earlier that the policy elements of this study do not exhaust those that might exist, nor do they necessarily include the most important. Further, the policy environments I have presented do not account for all the organizational, operational, or other important features of the schools they represent. They do not, for example, address the importance and centrality of curriculum, the way the school day is structured, or a host of other important school matters. They do not, then, exhaust what might be called the "cultures" of these schools (see Chapter 5).

Similarly, the commonalities identified below do not exhaust those that might exist, nor do they necessarily include the most important. They are those that are most manifest, most directly supported by the evidence, and those I found most telling about the nature and function of these policy environments.

It should also be noted that the policy elements of this study are not ranked in any order of power or significance. I assume that some elements are more important than others, and that some are more important in some schools than in others. I cannot yet defend those assumptions, and they are not fundamental to this work. However, the policy environment perspective does rest on the assumption, grounded in this study, that the nature of the relationship among policy elements is telling.

CONTEXTUALITY

There is one characteristic of all policy elements in all schools that must be understood. Policy elements are contextual, that is, they are as they are because of where they exist, and this is true regardless of whether or not the schools are successful. All schools have, for example, an ethos, and the way the ethos exists and is expressed in any school is different from the way it is in any other.

Each policy element, then, is a consequence in part of the nature and function of others and of the whole. For example, TPA means certain things by itself. It means this "plus more" when it becomes part of a larger constellation of policy elements. As it existed in each school in this study, it helped define governance, organizational control, socialization, leadership, and so on.

Because each policy element is expressed within a policy environment, any generic definition for policy element would be inadequate. A high degree of TPA, or a certain kind of leadership may be desirable for all teachers in all schools, but to try to attain them by copying the TPA in some schools would be ill-advised. Moreover, the introduction of change to achieve a certain kind of TPA (or leadership, or socialization— any kind of policy element) in schools without attention to their existing policy environments would be problematic. Policy elements develop differently in different relationships with other elements and are embedded deep in the fabric of a school. Externally imposed change aimed at achieving some "standard" ignores this reality.

Although this quality of contextuality is obvious on reflection, it must be highlighted as the characteristics of policy elements are discussed. When we attempt school reform without attention to the policy environment context in which the reform would be placed, we risk failure, and we risk doing damage to what already exists. This concern is discussed in Chapter 11, in which the focus is school change.

Other characteristics of policy elements are described below. Unlike contextuality, the characteristics to be discussed seem to be unique to good schools. They may in fact be a distinctive feature of good schools.

FEATURES OF POLICY ELEMENTS IN GOOD SCHOOLS

Interdependence

When I had completed most of the analysis from my studies of the schools, I drew inferences about the salient policy dimensions of each school I was studying. From the beginning, I sought to express those conclusions in descriptive sentences and phrases. When considering TPA in a school, for example, my intent was to generate summative statements that would describe TPA in an accurate, telling way. The policy element descriptors in each of the policy environment tables (see Tables 6.1, 7.1, and 8.1) embody this intent. For instance, TPA at Ruraldom Union High School (see Table 6.1) "covers many policy and program matters. It is exercised in collective manner and is central to the school's character and operations." On the other hand, TPA at Townston Regional High School (see Table 7.1) "covers many program and policy areas and is exercised through mandated representation on committees; TPA is valued, given the professional respect it reflects and earns. Policy-making role [of teachers] is secondary to teaching." TPA at Cityville is "exercised through representation schoolwide, collectively at the cluster level," and both "TPA and autonomy [are] potent."

After completing descriptive statements of several of the policy elements for one of the schools I was analyzing, I found I could predict the essential character of other policy elements with a surprising degree of accuracy. For example, after deriving summative statements about mission, ethos, and governance for Ruraldom, I found I could predict other policy elements. I could anticipate what leadership would be like, what would characterize organizational control, and so on. I had the same experience with the policy element statements for Townston and Cityville. This was disturbing. It all seemed too neat and contrived. Was I creating fiction? I decided to see what people in the schools I studied had to say about this. I checked with some teachers and staff of some of the schools, and they reported that my draft summation accurately depicted their experience of the schools.

I concluded that predictability was understandable, at least in the good schools I studied. I did not find this predictability in the less successful schools among the 18 I visited for the SSRP and for which I had constructed abbreviated policy environment outlines, but in-depth study and an observation-informed data base were lacking. The predictability of the policy elements of the three good enough schools was a function of a coherence, an integrity, an interdependence.

The interdependence of the policy elements should not have been a surprise to me. Early in my observations and document analyses I saw that practices I had initially perceived as isolated or idiosyncratic in fact fit school philosophy and policy. In Ruraldom, the practice might be socialization of new teachers, frequent and visible honoring of good student performance, or welcoming of a visitor. In Townston, it could be the constant presence of college recruiters, the steady publication of materials touting the school's success, or the bound, finished quality of the bulletin containing each semester's course offerings. At Cityville, the variety of students' dress and behavior were predictive of a wealth of policy elements.

Each of these and other practices did not just happen. There were policies that addressed these matters; they, in turn, were derived from the expressed belief that school self-concept made and maintained the desired essence of the school.

In Townston, the novel and seemingly odd membership of custodians on a committee on library use turned out to be consistent with policies valuing the inclusion of all staff in the day-to-day business of the school. Guidance counselors taught courses on occasion and were regular presenters in many courses. These practices gave life to the belief, expressed in the philosophy of the school, that a school good for young people and for the staff in them depended on the participation of all in establishing vision, direction, and norms for its operation.

At Cityville, a veteran teacher insisted without opposition that a new teacher adopt a particular approach to teaching a mathematical concept. Such apparently haughty directiveness fit the cluster's statement about the teaching of math. This, in turn, echoed both the school's philosophy about teaching practices and the TPA as seen in the school's clusters.

In the schools of this study, and perhaps in successful schools generally, policy environments are complex arrangements of parts in an integral relation to one another. A positive, upbeat ambience may have been common to all, but the experience of staff, students, and visitors was profoundly different in each. The quality of interdependence among policy elements was common to all.

Congruity

The policy environments of the subject schools functioned as gatekeepers for what each school was and could become. Herein lay another interesting paradox. As the narratives in Part II made clear, the elements of the policy environment were traceable, at least in part, to choices and decisions about the kind of school desired by the people in them. However, the capacity of the policy elements to function normatively as intended depended on their fit with other elements and the policy environment overall. Thus, a choice to do something was contingent on the existing policy environment. Changes introduced without attention to an existing policy environment risked failure.

The quality of congruity evident in policy elements in these schools underscores the importance of understanding the policy environment in coming to know a school. It teaches, for example, that the activities of school professionals and the consequences of their activities cannot be fully understood in terms of the manifest functions of schools—teaching, learning, and testing—or in lists of the apparent traits of effective schools. All these are embedded in, derived from, and shaped by the policy environment. To understand fully what teachers do, and to comprehend how a curriculum functions, one must look at the schools' full policy environment. Saranson (1971) taught as much when he admonished that efforts to change a curriculum independent of changing associated characteristic institutional features risks complete failure. Murnane (1980) cautioned similarly, observing that a major task for the improvement of schools was "to develop mechanisms for incorporating into the decision-making process information about the priorities of the key actors, and consequently about their likely behavioral responses." (p. 24).

Murnane anticipated the policy environment perspective and underscored the importance of educational philosophy. The belief among the school professionals of this study that ideals, beliefs, values, attitudes, knowledge claims, and moral authority made a difference in the way schools functioned was central to how the schools worked.

Philosophy can be conceived of in many ways, but if considered a combination of the fundamental general beliefs, concepts, attitudes, and values of an individual or group, then the professionals of the schools in this study invested mightily in forming educational philosophy. They recognized the importance of expressing their individual and collective beliefs and values about education and schooling and of reaching consensus about the institutional policies and professional practices those beliefs and values would require.

Intentionality

School professionals in this study saw themselves as actors in a policy environment with understandable norms and rules that they helped fashion. They did not see themselves as reacting, passive role bearers. Thus, the policy environments of the subject schools revealed successful schools as intentional rather than reflexive. They were as they were because significant actors in them helped to make them that way.

Teachers' positive self-perception in these schools was likely a function both of their high TPA and of the fact that they and their schools were efficacious. Teachers had a sense of influence over their destiny because they helped fashion what the schools did, and what they and others did in them: their exercise of this influence led to successful results.

Analysis of the policy environments of these schools told us that school characteristics made a difference for students and that teachers contributed to those characteristics. We should, therefore, be serious about holding teachers and other school professionals accountable for their schools' performance, only when these professionals have the authority to make their schools as they think they should be. It is off-base and, in fact, punitive to hold school professionals accountable when giving them little control over conditions that we know yield positive outcomes.

I began this chapter with claims informed by this study. I claimed that all schools have a policy environment, all policy environments are comprised of policy elements, and all policy elements are contextual. The policy environments of successful schools may be distinguished by the interdependence, the congruity, and the intentionality of their policy elements.

Because I did not set out to study policy environments as such, much less to conduct an experimental study of the policy environments of successful versus less successful schools, claims derived from this study are limited, some more than others. Claims about the policy environments of less-than-successful schools are certainly limited. However, my observations suggest that the policy environments of less successful schools can be expected to be quite different from those of successful schools. We can expect them to reflect different, sometimes contradictory beliefs and values, and to lack congruence between policies and practices. We and those who teach and learn in less successful schools would likely find few compelling, commonly shaped imperatives, and would be frustrated with these schools' imperviousness to change and improvement. To put it another way, we could expect that the policy environments of less-than-successful schools would be fragmented (not interdependent), incongruent, and unintentional. It is likely that there is a lack of fit between philosophy and practice in less successful schools.

The policy environments of the successful schools in this study, on the other hand, show explicit linkages among policy elements and between those elements and the policy environment. It is no surprise that the collection of these schools' policies—their policy environments—make their philosophy and practices clear and predictable. The philosophy-policy-practice connection, or lack of it, appears to be a telling feature of school quality and performance.

Chapter 11

The Policy Environment Perspective and School Change

Three questions regarding school change (Tye, 1987) are central to the work of reformers. Appropriate answers to them can enhance the efficacy of change and reform efforts. Those questions can be expressed as follows:

1. What organizational entity should be the basic unit and means for introducing a change?
2. Where should the basic unit be engaged in order initiate a change?
3. How should the basic unit be engaged to effect a change?

These questions did not motivate my study nor did they frame its major conclusions. They presented themselves as related and important to this study through my attempts to understand some of the features of the schools studied and to make sense of what I heard from school professionals about school reform efforts. The professionals were universally proud in their disdain for the dominant school improvement strategies and goals of the

1980s and early 1990s. They rejected as irrelevant reform efforts and goals that emanated from outside their schools, especially those from national commissions. They were not uninterested in making schools, especially theirs, better. Indeed, we have seen that they worked hard and constantly at improvement. However, they regarded outsiders and their prescriptions as uninformed, irrelevant, ineffectual, and perhaps dangerous in terms of their own schools. Outsiders did not, could not know their schools. How could they even pretend to know how to improve them? And to what end? They could destroy what the teachers worked so hard to achieve. Imperviousness, derision, and defensiveness to that which outsiders deemed "improvement" or "reform" best captured the teachers' views.

In retrospect, these reactions and views should not have come as a surprise. Teachers viewed the reform movements of the 1980s and many of today's reform initiatives—indeed, commanded reform generally—as condemnatory and punitive. Teachers' voice had often been excluded in diagnosing school ills and in prescribing remedies. Those diagnoses overblamed teachers for student failures more appropriately attributable to school system, or to social failures and ills.

My concern with the three questions stated above arose from my efforts to understand teachers' and other school professionals' views of school reform, as well as the place and function of policy elements in the schools. Changes in schools simply will not take hold if conditions surrounding change and reform evoke the sentiments I encountered. The policy environment perspective instructs how to avoid such conditions.

Where to Begin

The first question regarding school change seeks to identify that aspect of a school or school system that should constitute the basic unit of analysis and means of implementation when considering school change. Clearly, a complete answer to this question depends on the kind of change involved. Should it be an individual school? All schools serving the same grades? All schools in a district? All schools within a state? Is the proposed change curricular? Structural?

The question begs consideration of that which would ensure the greatest chance of success. This study suggests that the policy environment of the individual school is the key to most changes intended to improve the outcomes of teaching and learning. As noted earlier, all schools have policy environments. All policy environments are characterized by contextuality and, therefore, are sufficiently complex that change not attentive to them courts failure and, worse, could render successful schools less so. Thus, the policy environment perspective suggests that the basic unit of analysis and means of implementation when considering school change must be the individual school and its policy elements.

This does not mean that some changes cannot be effected through other units (e.g., individual classrooms, grade levels, school systems, a curriculum). Indeed, schools have the capacity to change dramatically in response to certain types of large scale, externally imposed changes. Cuban's work (1990, 1992a, 1992b) on school reform instructs us in this regard. Changes that expand, solidify, and entrench school bureaucracy—changes that apparently accommodate the sameness aspects of schools—seem to have strong and enduring effects. Overall, however, externally mandated changes to influence outcomes of teaching and learning have weak, ephemeral effects (Elmore & McLaughlin, 1988).

The record of school reform in the United States (see, for example, Cuban, 1990, 1992a, 1992b; Elmore & McLaughlin, 1988; Tyack, 1991) and the policy environment perspective teach us that commanded or imposed success (or excellence, or effectiveness, or total quality) in teaching and learning outcomes cannot endure, even if it appears to take effect initially. Nor can those on whom it is imposed be coerced for long into pursuing it. The schools depicted in this study teach us that change and success emerge as a function of the choices, goals, understandings, expectations, and norms created and shared by the stakeholders in the teaching-learning enterprise (Raywid, Tesconi, & Warren, 1985). In other words, change and success emerge in the light of school policy elements, policy environments, and their makers.

Let us consider teacher professional authority in this regard. It seems that everyone recognizes now that teachers have had little voice in making the policy environments through which they work, and as noted (see Chapter 4), school organizational structure reinforces this sorry state of affairs. A now widely endorsed remedy calls for increased teacher professional authority in schools, with more autonomy than has been the case (Levin, 1991). More TPA, we are told, will enhance teacher satisfaction, enhance the status of teachers, improve teacher and school performance, and make teaching more attractive to able young people. School reformers, it seems, have finally grasped what others have known for some time: use of worker expertise in shaping the workplace enhances performance, and employees accord legitimacy to and cooperate in the implementation of policies they have helped formulate.

The call for increased TPA is a good one. However, a move to effect more TPA could create enormous problems for teachers. As we have seen, TPA, whether it is great or small, broad or narrow, always resides within a unique and, in the successful schools of this study, delicately balanced constellation of policy elements. Change introduced by imposition or even collaboration, if it is inattentive to the existing policy environment, risks at least two negative outcomes: first, results counter to intentions— thus frustration and disdain for an otherwise valued reform; and secondly, an unintended change in the nature and function of the existing policy environment and, again, frustration and associated negative consequences.

To realize the worthy goal of more greater teacher professional authority, it will be necessary not only to have the mandate, but to carefully establish the kind and extent of TPA that would be appropriate for a particular school, given its policy elements and policy environment.

Where to Engage

The second important question about school change asks where one enters or engages the basic unit to enhance or to ensure realization of the change sought. Should it be through the curriculum? Through teaching and teachers? Through administration? Through the principal?

Again, the answer here depends in part on the nature of the change involved. However, the study addressed in this book tells us that changes aimed at improving the outcomes of schooling must be engaged through the policy environment of the individual school. Thus, that engagement must begin with an appropriate policy element or elements.

Which policy element to begin with and how many to consider must be addressed and decided at the individual school level. These matters can only be sufficiently addressed and appropriately decided after a study at the individual school level that results in an outline of the school's policy environment. The displayed policy environment, in turn, must be considered relative to the specific nature and function of the change intended.

Although not sufficient to a full understanding of a school and the place of its professionals in change, the exposure of policy elements and their relationships is basic and necessary to such understanding and to assessing where and how to implement change. School improvement is not likely to come about through command or through the emulation of seemingly effective or excellent schools. Schools are too complex; and because each school is unique, schools will not be moved to change without accommodations to their existing policy environments. The policy environment perspective indicates, then, that the path to sustained reform lies in strategies that attend to the unique policy elements of the each school.

How to Engage

The third question seeks the proper and efficacious way to engage the basic unit to achieve a valued change. As already discussed, realization of a valued change requires assessment of the potential fit of the proposed change with the existing policy elements and policy environment. Does the nature of the policy environment suggest that the change will fit with what is? Will the policy environment accept the change, or will the policy environment repel the change? Will the change maximize the strengths or the limitations of the existing policy environment? What must be done to the change and to the existing policy elements and policy environment to enhance the prospects of success for a valued and wanted change?

The necessary assessment requires the following three-step process:

1. The policy elements of a school must be identified and described.
2. The functions of the policy elements individually and as they are combined as a policy environment must be fully expressed and assessed.
3. A strategy that will make it likely that the change will be embraced must be created with all those who help shape and work in the policy environment.

Clearly, policy environments must become known. This is a relatively easy but time-consuming undertaking. The approach to this task requires, minimally, study, description, and assessment of the following:

• school physical environment
• mission and goal statements

- statements of institutional beliefs and principles
- statements of educational philosophy
- overall school atmosphere
- organizational structure
- governance arrangements
- formal and informal roles of significant actors
- teacher professional authority
- teacher autonomy
- lines of authority
- relationships between and among all groups
- relationships between positions of authority
- nature and function of socialization
- nature and extent of parental involvement
- school credibility with significant publics
- accreditation and other self studies
- minutes of standing and other committees
- school and third party claims
- policy documents, handbooks, and manuals.

It is probably the case that the policy environment of a successful school will be much easier to map and describe than that of a less successful school. As noted in the Postscript and in Chapter 10, the policy elements of a successful school are described as interdependent, congruous, and intentional. Thus, aspects of them will be predictable. The policy elements of less successful schools will lack integrity. They will be fragmented and without interdependence, congruity, and intentionality. Accordingly, school professionals and other significant actors in such schools will have much more to do than those in successful schools. Further, they will have to confront the task of deciding what they wish to make of their schools and what kinds of policies and practices will move them in that direction. Clearly, the making of policies that are interconnected will be an important step to achieving their goals.

The policy environment perspective indicates that change efforts succeed when they are compatible or reconcilable with a school's policy environment. Whether the attempt at reform originates internally or externally, whether it is major or minor, it is likely to fail unless it fits with or can be accommodated by the prevailing policy environment. This perspective suggests that it is lack of attention to policy environments, not an intractability among school professionals, that may be faulted when attempts at reform fail.

Seeking to change a school is not the only reason for exposing its policy environment. Simply knowing the policy environment of a school would be instructive for the people who must study and work in it. It could also serve as an important basis for informing a school's publics. Consider that Tables 6.1, 7.1, and 8.1 sketch an image suggestive of the essential character, internal relations, and operations of the schools depicted. One need not be familiar with any of the schools to grasp through the Tables a sense of what each is like. One could predict with some accuracy, for example, what meetings of the faculty are like, what kinds of conversations are likely to be heard in the faculty lounges, and what it feels like to be a teacher in these schools. So, one of the most important functions of a policy environment is to convey something essential about the character of a school. We have noted that understanding a policy environment is not sufficient for a full understanding of a school. It is, however, necessary.

Epilogue

Policy environment is my term for the building-level, system-like arrangement of logically and functionally related, salient policy-based dimensions of the schools in this study. These policy elements were occasioned in part by the decisions of the professionals in these schools.

The policy environments of the schools evoked the policy environment perspective which, among other things, offers insight into how school uniformity and uniqueness interact; instructs about a school's readiness for change; and identifies access points for particular changes in a school. This perspective suggests that it is a lack of attention to policy environments, not intractability among school professionals, that may be faulted when attempts at school reform fail.

The policy environment perspective may qualify as "grounded theory" (Glasser & Strauss, 1967). I collected, categorized, and analyzed information for this study consistent with the demands of grounded theory. The analysis suggested relationships among school policy elements chosen for study; and these

153

relationships, in turn, suggested patterns of policy elements—or policy environments—that became means to understand the schools and other matters. Policy environment was the core theoretical construct that grew out of research on the three high schools. Supporting conceptual categories, such as *policy element* and its properties, that were generated from evidence became foundational to the development of this construct (Glasser & Strauss, 1967).

This study is limited by the constraints of ethnographic studies generally; the policy environment perspective as grounded theory is correspondingly limited.

One shortcoming stands out in retrospect: I lacked the foresight to collect enough information about some of the less successful schools that I visited for the SSRP. Otherwise, I would have been in a position to document their full policy environments and to compare and contrast them with those of the three successful schools. Claims derived from this study would then have been put to a first test.

It is the case, nevertheless, that claims made herein are open to testing. The policy environments of schools can be mapped. They can become known. School professionals can be trained to do this in their schools, and I believe they should. In turn, the policy environments of high schools documented as successful, and of those not successful, could be subjected to comparative analysis. Tests of my claims about the nature and function of policy environments and the policy environment perspective could then be arranged. Accordingly, the value and worth of this study and its claims could be assessed relative to its "generative promise" (Peskin, 1993).

Some of the major claims of this study relate to school change and reform. Because social problems in the United States have always evoked the public school as remediator of those problems, we have seen continuing calls for more schooling and more school reform. And, because social problems are essentially national, reform initiatives have been as well.

There are limits and dangers to this apparently logical link. The limits have to do with any organizational entity accepting reform that is mandated elsewhere, and with the actual inability of some policy environments to accommodate some changes. The danger is that as we continue to set schools up for failure, the same privileged citizens who could make our schools instruments for social as well as individual betterment will instead, feeling disenfranchised and disillusioned, abandon them; a state of affairs we seem to be rapidly approaching.

The policy environment perspective teaches us a great deal about all this. Above all else, it confirms that mandated change shifts authority from the local school and shapes a bureaucratic model that leaves teachers, principals, and local citizens more accountable but less empowered. Then, most unfairly, it is the front line people, trying their best, who are faulted if the "one size fits all" plans cannot be made to work.

Commanded reform and centralization encourage individuals to look outside themselves to agencies and others as the arbiters of decisions. The consequence is the accrual of power by offices and officers distant from and unknowledgeable about the local context. Centralized mandates encourage bureaucratic compliance, discourage leadership and initiative, and substitute an impersonal system that makes it inane to hold anyone accountable. Reforms of this sort perpetuate fictions about the power of the schools and reinforce tendencies to ignore other ways of reforming either society or schools.

As noted throughout much of this book, the policy environment perspective revealed that the successful schools of this study were in part constructed: They were what they were because the significant actors in them intended to make them that way. Accordingly, the policy environment perspective revealed that schools can be made what we want them to be and that school professionals can be made truly accountable.

The professionals of the schools in this study expressed their individual and collective beliefs, ideals, values, attitudes, knowledge claims, and moral views in institutional philosophies. They translated those philosophies into policies. Those policies committed them to certain practices. All of this was known to the schools' various publics. They could legitimately hold the schools and the professionals in them accountable. School policy as a mediating variable between philosophy and practice abhors mandated change and begs for attention as the locus for understanding a school, its limits, and its possibilities.

Appendix 1

THE NOMINATION FORM
SECONDARY SCHOOL RECOGNITION PROGRAM
COVER SHEET

School Name _____ District _____
Principal's Name (Mrs. Miss. Ms. Mr. Dr.)_____
Address_____
    _____
    _____

Telephone Number ( )   Congressional District
I have reviewed the information contained in this form and, to the best
of my knowledge, it is accurate.

        _____   _____
        (Principal's signature)   Date

* * * * * * * * * * * * * * * * * * *

Superintendent's Name (Mrs. Miss Ms. Mr. Dr.)_____
Address_____
    _____
    _____

Telephone Number ( )_____

I have reviewed the information contained in this form and, to the best
of my knowledge, it is accurate.

        _____   _____
        Superintendent's Signature   Date

School Board President's Name   (Mrs. Miss Ms. Mr. Dr.)_____
Address_____

_____

_____

Telephone Number (   )_____Congressional District_____

I have reviewed the information contained in this form and, to the best of my knowledge, it is accurate.

_____   _____

(School Board Presidents's signature)   Date

I. SCHOOL AND DISTRICT CHARACTERISTICS

1.   Which grades are included in your school, and how many students are enrolled in each? ____9th ____10th ____11th ____12th _____ Total
2.   How many students are enrolled in the district?_____
3.   How many schools are in the district?_____ Elementary Schools _____ Junior High or Middle Schools _____ High Schools _____ Total
4.   How many people reside in the district served by your school?
_____
5.   In general, how would you classify the district?_____Rural _____Suburban_____ Urban
6.   What is the ethnic composition of the student body in your school? _____ % White _____ % Black _____ % Asian _____ %Hispanic_____ % Native American _____% Other

Does your school have a sizeable group of recent immigrants or refugees?_____

7.   What percentage of the students in your school come from low income families?_____ Please indicate how you determined this number.
8.   Please describe briefly any significant changes that have occurred in these figures during the last 3-5 years.

9.   What are the primary educational needs of the particular group of students served by your school? Please indicate how these needs were determined and whether there are ongoing procedures for reviewing their relevance.

10. Does your school have any entrance requirements such as performance on an entrance exam? If so, please describe.

   _____

11. Please indicate the number of staff in each of the following positions:

	Full-time	Part-time
Administrators	_____	_____
Classroom teachers	_____	_____
Teacher aides	_____	_____
Counselors	_____	_____
Subject area specialists	_____	_____
(e.g. Reading specialists)	_____	_____
Library and other media professionals	_____	_____
Social workers	_____	_____
Security officers	_____	_____
Food service personnel	_____	_____
Clerical	_____	_____

   Have there been any significant changes in any of these numbers in the last three years?_____

12. How long has the principal been in his/her position?_____
13. How long have the other administrators been in their positions?

   _____

* * * * * * * * * * * * * * * * * * *

II. PROGRAMS, POLICIES, AND PRACTICES
The items in this section are intended to gather information about the ways the 14 attributes of success are reflected in the programs, policies, and practices in your school. The last item in this section invites you, if appropriate, to describe other features of your school that contribute to its success.

In completing this section of the form, please highlight those elements of your school programs, policies, and practices that are particularly important in meeting the student needs described in the previous section.

1. CLEAR ACADEMIC GOALS

What are the overall instructional goals of your school? How were they identified? How are they communicated to the students? Teachers? Parents?

2. HIGH EXPECTATIONS FOR STUDENTS

In the chart below, please indicate the minimum graduation requirements for English, Math, Social Studies, Science, and Foreign Language

	1 year	2 years	3 years	4 years
English	_____	_____	_____	_____
Math	_____	_____	_____	_____
Social Studies	_____	_____	_____	_____
Science	_____	_____	_____	_____
Foreign Language	_____	_____	_____	_____

What other requirements must be met for graduation?

In the chart below, please indicate the number of students enrolled in advanced study or honors classes in English, Math, Social Studies, Science, and Foreign Language. Also, please indicate how advanced study in defined.

	No. in advanced study	Definition of advanced study
English	_____	_____
Math	_____	_____
Social Studies	_____	_____
Science	_____	_____
Foreign Language	_____	_____

In general, are students encouraged to complete course work that exceeds the basic requirements? If so, how? Approximately how many students do exceed these requirements? In what areas?

Does your school have any programs that concentrate on developing student study skills? If so, please describe them. How many students do they serve?

Does your school have any programs that provide remediation in basic skills or other content areas? If so, please describe them and indicate how students are selected for them.

3. ORDER AND DISCIPLINE

Please summarize your school's overall approach to discipline. Are there any special procedures or programs to maintain order and discipline? If so, please describe them and, as appropriate, indicate the number of students served by them.

4. REWARDS AND INCENTIVES FOR STUDENTS

Aside from grades, does your school have procedures for recognizing outstanding student accomplishments in course work as well as other school activities? If so, please describe them.

5. REGULAR AND FREQUENT MONITORING OF STUDENT PROGRESS

Other than report cards, does your school have regular procedures for notifying students and parents of student progress and problems in coursework? If so, please describe them.

Are there procedures for monitoring student development and participation in other areas? If so, please describe them.

6. OPPORTUNITIES FOR MEANINGFUL STUDENT RESPONSIBILITY AND PARTICIPATION

What opportunities exist for student participation in school governance?

What opportunities exist for student participation in school-related community activities?

Please describe your school's program of co-curricular activities (e.g. clubs, intramural sports). Approximately what percentage of the student body is served by these activities?

7. TEACHER EFFICACY

What opportunities exist for teacher input in decisions about (a) instruction, (b) curriculum, (c) discipline policy, (d) teacher evaluation, (e) other activities?

Does your school have an ongoing staff development program? If so, please describe it, and discuss how it is planned. (Please do not include district level or other activities not specifically developed for your school.) Are there opportunities for teachers to complete advanced study in the content areas, reading instruction or instruction in other communication skills?

8. REWARDS AND INCENTIVES FOR TEACHERS

Does your school have formal procedures for evaluating teachers? If so, please describe them, including the feedback mechanisms.

Are there formal procedures for recognizing excellent teachers? Are there special rewards or incentives available for them? If so, please describe them.

9. CONCENTRATION ON ACADEMIC LEARNING TIME

What policies and procedures does your school and/or district have to ensure effective use of time available for teaching and learning in the academic core.

Does your school have a formal policy on homework? If so, please summarize it. How is it enforced?

10. POSITIVE SCHOOL CLIMATE

In general, how would you describe the climate of your school? What has been done to create this climate? Were these things planned or unplanned?

11. ADMINISTRATIVE LEADERSHIP

Aside from the regular staff meetings and routine memoranda and announcements, are there regular opportunities and procedures, formal or informal, for communication between the principal and the staff? If so, please describe them. Please highlight those that focus on school-wide instructional issues.

What opportunities are there for communication and coordination among other building administrators and teachers?

In what other ways does your building principal demonstrate instructional and administrative leadership?

12. WELL-ARTICULATED CURRICULUM

What procedures are followed to ensure proper sequencing and to reduce overlap in the various content areas?

Are there procedures for review of content and sequence across grade levels? If so, please describe them.

Are there regular opportunities for planning and coordination of content among teachers on the high school level and teachers on the middle school or junior high school level? If so, please describe them.

13. EVALUATION FOR INSTRUCTIONAL IMPROVEMENT

Does your school have regular procedures for evaluating the success of instructional programs and the effectiveness of the organizational structure? If so, please describe them. When was the most recent evaluation completed? Who participated?

How are the results of the evaluation communicated to the community?

Please provide some examples of ways the results of the evaluation have been used to improve school programs, policies, and practices.

14. COMMUNITY SUPPORT AND INVOLVEMENT

Please describe briefly the relationships with the community served by your school. Please describe any opportunities for parent participation.

Are there opportunities for participation by other groups in the community e.g., civic and business associations? If so, please describe them.

Is the school available for use by community groups for educational or other programs? If so, please describe the activities.

Please use this space to describe elements of your school's programs, policies, and practices which, in your judgment, are important in understanding the success of your school and which are not described previously.

III. PROGRESS TOWARD EXCELLENCE

1. As you look back over the last 3-5 years, what conditions and changes have contributed most to the overall success of your school? In answering this question, please feel free to expand your answers to previous questions and to introduce any new information that you feel is important in understanding your school.

2. Establishing and maintaining successful schools frequently involves overcoming a variety of obstacles and impediments. What problems has your school faced during the last 3-5 years and how have you overcome them?

IV. INDICATORS OF SUCCESS

1. Aside from regular evaluation of student performance, does your school have formal procedures for measuring student achievement? If so, please describe them, and in a form appropriate for your school, indicate the results from the last three evaluation periods.

2. Does your school, district, or State have a minimum competency testing program? If so, please describe, in a format appropriate for your school, the results from the last three evaluation periods.

3. Of the students who graduated last year, approximately how many:

        Enrolled in a four-year college or university_____
        Enrolled in a community college   _____
        Enrolled in vocational training   _____
        Enlisted in the military   _____
        Found full-time employment   _____
        Found part-time employment   _____

Have any of these rates changed significantly (i.e. by more than 10%) in the last 3-5 years? If so, please describe the changes and the reasons for them.

4. Of the students who went on to some form of post-secondary education or training, how many received scholarships or other awards? Has this number changed significantly in the last 3-5 years?

5. Please indicate your school's performance last year in the following areas:

        Daily student attendance _____
        Daily teacher attendance _____
        Number of drop-outs   _____
        Number of suspensions   _____   _____ In school
                                             _____ Out of school
        Number of other exclusions _____

Have any of these rates changed significantly (i.e. by more than 10%) in the past 3-5 years?

6. Please describe any recent awards received in your school for outstanding programs and teacher performance.

7. Please describe any awards or recognition received by your students in academic, vocational, or co-curricular competitions.

Appendix 2

School Name_____Code____
City_____State_____
Visitor_____
Date of Visit _____

SITE VISIT GUIDE

1. THE TEACHERS

(a). Please describe the teachers' perceptions of the current state of the school. Do they think it is a good school? How does it feel to them? (i.e. friendly, warm, exciting, boring, etc.)

(b). Do teachers think they have a meaningful role in planning and decision making? Please cite examples.

167

(c). Do teachers feel that they have ample opportunity for communication and planning about curriculum development? Instructional issues? Other program or policy issues? Do these opportunities extend across subject areas and/or grade levels? Please cite examples.

(d). Do teachers feel that their efforts and accomplishments (in planning, in program development, in teaching, etc.) are recognized and appreciated? If so, how and by whom?

2. THE STUDENTS
(a). Do students think this is a good school? Why? How does the school feel to them? (i.e. warm, friendly, exciting, boring, intimidating, etc.) Do they feel that there are adults with whom they can talk or from whom they can seek advice? Are there teachers they admire and respect?

(b). What do students seem not to like about the school?

(c). Please describe students' impressions of what is expected of them (work expectations and behavioral expectations). Do they feel that the amount and type of work they are expected to do is reasonable? How much time to they spend on it during the day and after school?

(d). Do students see any opportunities to influence school programs and/or policy? If so, please describe them.

3. SPECIAL SERVICE PERSONNEL (Reading Teachers, Counselors etc.)

(a). Do these individuals perceive that their roles and functions are adequately integrated into the regular school program? How? (e.g. Note approximate percentage of time spent with students vs. time spent on administrative duties.)

(b). Do the specialists feel that they have ample opportunity for communication with subject area teachers, parents? How is this accomplished?

4. PARENTS/COMMUNITY

(a). Do parents (and other members of the community) think this is a good school? Why? How does this school feel to them? (i.e. intimidating, friendly, warm, exciting, boring, etc.)

(b). Do they feel they have adequate access to the principal and staff? What are some examples of positive interactions between the school and the community?

5. THE PRINCIPAL

(a). Please describe the principal's assessment of the current state of the school. What is she/he really excited about?

(b). What is the principal doing to sustain improvements and what is he/she doing to solve problems?

(c). Describe the principals' vision of the future of the school. How does he/she plan on realizing it?

6. INFORMAL SETTINGS

(a). Please describe the general nature of the interactions among students and among students and adults in the corridors, in the cafeteria, and in other gathering places inside and outside of the building.

(b). Please describe the atmosphere of the school while classes are in session (i.e. noise level in the corridor, interruptions in classroom routines, etc.)

7. FORMAL INSTRUCTIONAL SETTINGS

Please describe the activities and instructional settings you observed during your visit. (Are there examples of team teaching, individualized instruction, uses of educational technology or media, interdisciplinary instruction, peer tutoring, etc.) Please cite examples.

8. PHYSICAL FACILITIES

Please describe the overall condition of the building and grounds. Are they clean and well-maintained? Is there much graffiti? Is student work displayed in the corridors or other central locations?

9. THE SUPERINTENDENT (OR LEA OTHER OFFICIAL)

Please summarize any portion of your conversation that may be pertinent to understanding what contributes to the school's success.

10. ADDITIONAL INFORMATION

References

Abbott, M. (1969). Hierarchical impediments to innovation in educational organizations. In F. Carver & T. Sergiovanni (Eds.), *Organizations and human behavior: Focus on schools* (pp. 17-33). New York: McGraw- Hill.

Abbott, M., & Caracheo, F. (1988). Power, authority, and bureaucracy. In N. Boyan (Ed.), *Handbook of research on educational administration* (pp. 239-257). New York: Longman.

Averch, H.A., Carroll, S.J., Donaldson, T.S., Kiesling, H.J., & Pincus, J. (1972). *How effective is schooling? A critical review and synthesis of research findings.* (Prepared for the President's Commission on School Finance.) Santa Monica, CA: The Rand Corporation.

Bossert, S. (1988). School effects. In N. Boyan (Ed.), *Handbook of research on educational administration* (pp. 340-357). New York: Longman.

Brookover, W.B., Beady, C., Flood, P., Schweitzer, J., & Wisenbaker, J. (1979). *School social systems and school achievement: Schools can make a difference.* South Hadley, MA: J. F. Bergin (Distributed by Praeger, New York).

171

Brookover, W.B., Beamer, L., Efthim, H., Hathaway, D., Lezotte, L., Miller, S., Passalacqua, J., & Tornatzky, L. (1982). *Creating effective schools. An inservice program for enhancing school learning climate and achievement.* Holmes Beach, FL: Learning Publications.

Brookover, W.B., & Lezotte, L.W. (1977). *Changes in school characteristics coincident with changes in students achievement.* (Executive Summary). East Lansing: Michigan State University, Institute for Research on Teaching.

Bryk, A.S., Lee, V.E., & Smith, J.L. (1990). High school organization and its effects on teachers and students: An interpretive summary of the research. In W.H. Clune & J.F. Witte (Eds.), *Choice and control in American education: Vol. I.* Philadelphia: Falmer.

Carnegie Foundation for the Advancement of Teaching. (1988, September). *Teacher involvement in decision making.* New York: Carnegie Foundation for the Advancement of Teaching.

Cohen, M. (1983). Instructional management and social conditions in effective schools. In A. Odden & D. Webb (Eds.), *School finance and school improvement strategies for the 1980s* (pp. 76-90). Cambridge, MA: Bolinger.

Coleman, J.S., Campbell, E., Hobson, C., McPartland, J., Mood, A., Weinfeld, F., & Yonk, R. (1966). *Equality of educational opportunity.* Washington, DC: US Government Printing Office.

Cuban, L. (1990). Reforming, again, again, and again. *Educational Researcher, 19,* 3-13.

Cuban, L. (1992a). What happens to reforms that last?: The case of the junior high school. *American Educational Research Journal, 29*(2) 227-251.

Cuban, L. (1992b). Why some reforms last: The case of the kindergarten. *American Journal of Educational Research, 100*(3) 166-194.

Cusick, P.A. (1983). *The egalitarian ideal and the American high school: Studies of three high schools.* New York: Longman.

Edmonds, R. (1979a). Effective schools for the urban poor. *Educational Leadership, 37*(1) 15-24.

Edmonds, R. (1979b). Some schools work and more can. *Social Policy, 9,* 28-32.

Edmonds, R. (1980). *Developing effective schools.* West Hartford, CT: New England Teacher Corps.

Edmonds, R. (1982). Programs of school improvement: An overview. *Educational Leadership, 40,* 4-11.

Elmore, R.F., & Associates. (1990). *Restructuring schools: The next generation of educational reform.* San Francisco: Jossey-Bass.

Elmore, R.F. & McLaughlin, M.W. (1988). *Steady work: Policy, practice and the reforming of American education.* Santa Monica, CA: The Rand Corporation.

Ginsberg, A. et al. (1970). *Title I of ESEA: Problems and Prospects.* Washington, DC: The Department of Health, Education and Welfare.

Glasser, B., & Strauss, A. (1967). *The discovery of grounded theory: Strategies for qualitative research.* Chicago: Aldine.

Goodlad, J. (1984) *A place called school.* New York: McGraw-Hill.

Grant, G. (1988). *The world we created at Hamilton High.* Cambridge, MA: Harvard University Press.

Guba, E. (1984). The effect of definitions of policy on the nature and outcomes of policy analysis. *Educational Leadership, 42,* 63-70.

Hallinger, P., & Murphy, J. (1987). Instructional leadership in the school context. In W. Greenfield (Ed.), *Instructional leadership: Concepts, issues and controversies* (pp. 179-182). Boston: Allyn and Bacon.

Hanson. E.M. (1991). *Educational administration and organizational behavior* (3rd ed.) Boston: Allyn and Bacon.

Hanushek, E.A. (1972). *Longitudinal surveys of educational effects.* Washington, DC: Council of Economic Advisors.

Holmes, M. (1989). School effectiveness: From research to implementation to improvement. In M. Holmes, K. Leithwood, & D. Musella (Eds.), *Educational policy for effective schools* (pp. 3-30). New York: Teachers College Press.

Jencks, C., Smith, M., Ackland, H., Bane, M.J., Cohen, D., Gintis, H., Heyns, B., & Michelson, S. (1972). *Inequality: A reassessment of the effects of family and schooling in America.* New York: Basic Books.

Klitgaard, R. & Hall, G. (1973). *A statistical search for unusually effective schools.* Santa Monica, CA: The Rand Corporation.

Levin, H.M. (1991). *Building school capacity for effective teacher empowerment: Applications to elementary schools with at-risk students.* New Brunswick, NJ: Rutgers University, Center for Policy Research in Education.

Lightfoot, S.L. (1983). *The good high school: Portraits of character and culture.* New York: Basic Books.

Lou Harris & Associates. (1985). *Metropolitan life poll of the American teacher.* New York: Author.

Metz, M. (1986). *Different by design: The context and character of three magnet schools.* New York: Routledge & Kegan Paul.

Murnane, R.J. (1980, December). *Interpreting the evidence on school effectiveness* (Working Paper No. 830). New Haven, CT: Yale University, Institution for Social and Policy Studies.

National Commission on Excellence in Education. (1983). *A nation at risk. The imperative for reform.* Washington, D.C.: US Government Printing Office.

National Education Association. (1986, March). *The learning workplace: An introduction to the NEA research on the conditions and resources of teaching* (Preliminary Report). Washington, DC: NEA.

Page, R. (1990). Cultures and curricula: differences between and within schools. *Educational Foundations, 4*(1).

Peskin, A. (1993). The goodness of qualitative research. *Educational Researcher, 22*(2), 23-29.

Pink, W.T. (1987). In search of exemplary junior high schools. In W.T. Pink & G. Noblit (Eds.), *Schooling in social context* (pp. 218-249). Norwood, NJ: Ablex.

Powell, A., Farrar, E., & Cohen, D. (1986). *The shopping mall high school. Winners and losers in the educational marketplace.* Boston: Houghton Mifflin.

Purkey, S.C., & Smith, M.S. (1983). Effective schools: A review. *Elementary School Journal, 83,* 427-452.

Ralph, J.H., & Fennessey, J. (1983). Science or reform: Some questions about the effective schools model. *Phi Delta Kappan, 66*(10), 689-694.

Raywid, M.A., Tesconi, C. & Warren, D. (1985) *Pride and promise: Schools of excellence for all the people.* Westbury, NY: American Educational Studies Association.

Rutter, M., Maugham, B., Montimore, P., Ousten, J. & Smith, A. (1979). *Fifteen thousand hours: Secondary schools and their effects on children.* Cambridge, MA: Harvard University Press.

Saranson, S. (1971). *The culture of the school and the problem of change.* Boston: Allyn and Bacon.

Schein, E.H. (1985). *Organizational culture and leadership.* San Francisco: Jossey-Bass.

Squires, D.A., Huitt, W.G.,& Segars, J.K. (1983). *Effective schools and classrooms: A research-based perspective.* Washington, DC: Association for Supervision and Curriculum Development.

Teacher education reports. (1986, April 24). 8(8).

TEMPO. (1968). *Surveys and analyses of results from Title I funding for compensatory education.* Santa Barbara, CA: General Electric Co.

Tyack, D. (1991). Public school reform: Policy talk and institutional practice. *American Journal of Education, 100,* 1-19.

Tye, B.B. (1987). The deep structure of schooling. *Phi Delta Kappan, 69*(4), 281-285.

Weber, G. (1971). *Inner city children can be taught to read: Four successful schools.* Washington, DC: Council for Basic Education.

Wilson, B.L., & Corcoran, T.B. (1988). *Visions of excellence in American public education: Successful secondary schools.* Philadelphia: Falmer.

Author Index

Subject Index